OLAV HACKSTEIN

Apposition and Nominal Classification in Indo-European and Beyond

ÖSTERREICHISCHE AKADEMIE DER WISSENSCHAFTEN
PHILOSOPHISCH-HISTORISCHE KLASSE
SITZUNGSBERICHTE, 798. BAND

VERÖFFENTLICHUNGEN ZUR IRANISTIK
HERAUSGEGEBEN VON BERT G. FRAGNER UND VELIZAR SADOVSKI

NR. 56

OLAV HACKSTEIN

APPOSITION AND NOMINAL CLASSIFICATION IN INDO-EUROPEAN AND BEYOND

Verlag der
Österreichischen Akademie
der Wissenschaften

Wien 2010

ÖAW

Vorgelegt von w. M. BERT G. FRAGNER
in der Sitzung am 11. Dezember 2009

Die verwendete Papiersorte ist aus chlorfrei gebleichtem Zellstoff hergestellt, frei von säurebildenden Bestandteilen und alterungsbeständig.

ISBN 978-3-7001-6803-4

Druck: Ferdinand Berger & Söhne Ges.m.b.H., A-3580 Horn

http://hw.oeaw.ac.at/6803-4
http://verlag.oeaw.ac.at

CONTENTS

1. The hypothesis: Close apposition as the source of nominal classifiers[1]

Among the world's languages, we frequently find languages that use noun classifiers. According to a canonical definition, noun classifiers are free morphemes standing next to the noun, and classifying it according to some of its inherent functions or semantic properties.[2] Nominal classifier systems are found inter alia in a number of Austronesian languages, numerous Australian languages, and some Mesoamerican languages.[3] Consider the following two examples, cited from the Australian language Yidiny and from Jacaltec, a Mayan language.

Yidiny	***minya***	*gangu:l*
(Pama-Nyungan, Australian)	**animal.**CLF	wallaby
	(Wilkins 2000: 166)	
Jacaltec	***naj***	*Pel*
(Kanjobalan, Mayan)	**man.**CLF	Peter
	(Craig 1986: 264)	

---

1 This monograph is a sequel to a previous study published in the Festschrift for Werner Winter (Hackstein 2003: 131-152). An earlier version of sections 1 and 2 of the present monograph was presented on June 11, 2003 at the 22nd East Coast Indo-European Conference at Harvard University. Grateful acknowledgment is made to the Deutsche Forschungsgemeinschaft for a travel grant which enabled me to attend this conference. A later version was presented to the 26th annual conference of the Deutsche Gesellschaft für Sprachwissenschaft at Mainz on February 27, 2004. I wish to thank the audiences of both conferences for stimulating discussion. Many thanks also to Patience Epps, Orin Gensler, Tom Güldemann, Albertine Hagenbuchner, and David Stifter for answers to my queries, and to other informants who helped me in gathering data for this study: K. Philip Augustin (Malayalam), Renate Bagossy (Hungarian), Hans Harder and Carmen Brandt (Bengali), Petri Kallio (Finnish), Zulajkhat Mallaeva (Avar). Finally, thanks to an anonymous reviewer for additional valuable comments. Any errors are, of course, my responsibility alone.

2 Cf. Craig (1994: 566), Wilkins (2000: 149), Aikhenvald (2000: 81-84, 307-330).

3 For a map showing the areal occurrence of noun classifier systems, see Aikhenvald (2000: 97).

In the Yidiny example, we find the generic classifier 'animal', immediately followed by the specific noun 'wallaby'. Note that the classifier *minya* still has the status of an independent lexeme; that is, it may also occur independently without an accompanying specific noun, meaning just 'animal'. In the example cited from Jacaltec, the classifier *naj* is also still a free morpheme, but contrary to Yidiny, the underlying lexeme, the Jacaltec word denoting 'man', *winaj*, has been phonetically reduced. What is important for our purposes is that the Yidiny and Jacaltec noun classifiers have clearly arisen from independent lexemes, and that the classifier constructions have arisen from close appositions. Aikhenvald (2000: 86f. fn. 5) is entirely justified in remarking that generic-specific combinations of the Australian kind such as 'fish flounder', 'plant potato', 'animal dog' are a frequent historical source of noun classification devices. Nominal classifiers are known to frequently result from grammaticalizations of nouns belonging to semantic subgroups such as A) kinship nouns, and nouns denoting humans (man, woman) and higher animates; B) generic (or superordinate) nouns (Aikhenvald 2000: 353). In light of such semantically transparent generic-specific constructions which represent emergent classifier systems, it is not surprising that syntactic phenomena such as close apposition are to be counted among the potential sources of noun classifiers.

In the present monograph, I will present more evidence to substantiate the assumption of diachronic connections between close appositions and noun classifiers. In particular, close appositions and noun classifiers can be shown to share certain syntactic, semantic and functional peculiarities.

First, I will argue that in close appositions, the ordering of the generic and the specific noun is not random. There is a tendency for head-final languages to postpose the generic noun (*wallaby - animal*), and for head-initial languages to prepose the generic noun (*animal - wallaby*). As we will see, the relationship between word order and pre- versus postposing of the generic noun is often mirrored in the ordering of grammaticalized noun classifiers.

In the second part, I will tackle the question of whether an NP involving a close apposition has an internal dependency structure—that is, what (if anything) counts as the "head". I will recast this question, preferring to speak in terms of the concept of semantic subordination. I will argue that there is indeed an internal dependency structure which is purely semantic. A sequence of specific noun plus generic noun like 'lion animal' or a member-class sequence like 'Richard king' equals a sequence of hyponym plus hyperonym or of subordinate plus superordinate noun. Conversely, a sequence of generic plus specific can be rephrased as hyperonym plus hyponym or superordinate noun plus subordinate noun. The underlying semantic dependency is expressed syntactically in two ways: the adjacency of the hyperonym and its corresponding hyponym, and the relocation of hyponyms depending on the branching direction.

Finally, I will apply my results to non-Indo-European languages with grammaticalized classifier systems. Two important principles that will emerge in the course of this study are the semantically driven relocation of relative hyponyms (§§3.1.1.1, 3.1.2, 3.2.2, 6) and the adjacency constraint, applying to noun classifiers and close appositions alike (§ 7.2).

The insights of sections §1-8 will open the way to a better understanding of Indo-European appositional collocations made up of numeral plus noun. As will emerge in §9, ancient Indo-European languages sporadically illustrate the transition of free appositional lexemes to syntactically governed words signifying classifiers, thus attesting the full scale of development leading from free collocations to syntactic constructions.

Most languages that have developed noun-classifier systems are non-Indo-European. Nonetheless, Indo-European languages can contribute to the question of the development of noun classifiers in at least two respects:

First, closer inspection reveals that ancient Indo-European languages have in some cases begun to conventionalize certain noun-noun appositional syntagms. Significantly, these constructions can be shown to serve discourse functions that are strikingly similar to those found with noun classifiers, e.g., highlighting, referencing/anaphora, individuation, etc., see below §8.2.

Second, a very few Indo-European languages have taken the extra step and have developed such appositional syntagms into true classifier systems. These are all modern Indo-Aryan languages such as Bengali and particularly Assamese, e.g., Bengali *śromik-car-jon* [labourer-four-person] 'the four labourers' (Dasgupta 1983: 20), Assamese *manuɦ-zɒn* [man-DEF.HUMAN.CLF] 'the man' (Goswami & Tamuli 2003: 417). The human classifier employed by both Bengali and Assamese is etymologically identical with Sanskrit and Vedic *jánaḥ* 'person'. The assumption that noun phrases such as Assamese *manuɦ-zɒn* 'the man' are to be derived from erstwhile noun-apposition phrases like *'man-person' is supported by instances such as Vedic *mā́nuṣo jánaḥ* '(hu)man being/person' (RV 6.2.3c), which provides an etymologically near-perfect[4] match for the Assamese expression.

Both these observations provide further support for the postulated evolutionary links between close appositions and noun classifiers.

2. Head-final postposing and head-initial preposing of close appositions in Indo-European and beyond

Turning to the first part of the investigation, which will be descriptive, I will document some Indo-European and non-Indo-European analogues to the Australian generic-specific construction.

2.1. Head-final word order and postposing of the generic noun

In section §2.1, I exemplify the postposing of the generic or less specific noun for languages with left-branching NP level and (mostly[5]) OV word order, comparing ancient Indo-European languages and modern non-Indo-European languages. As we will see, in both groups the basic ordering conforms to the pattern of specific plus generic. In other words, in such languages the default position of the generic appositive noun is **after** the referent.

The left-hand column in the tabular list below contains the ancient Indo-European material. I cite examples from Anatolian, Tocharian, Italic, Greek, and Sanskrit. All these languages belong to the SOV type in their oldest attested stages and tend to postpose single-word appositions to their accompanying nouns. Tocharian and Hittite are the most rigid; Vedic, Latin and Greek are less rigid; but they all quite consistently attest to a postposing scheme for **old** names, i.e. theonyms, zoological and botanical terms. This increases the chance that we are dealing with true archaisms, and minimizes the probability that the postposing is merely a synchronic stylistic option.

The right-hand column presents comparable material from modern non-Indo-European OV languages. The postposing of appositions in these verb-final languages is again very prevalent, and readily yields syntactic

---

4 It must be noted that Vedic *mā́nuṣa-*, despite its adjectival origin, shows substantive-like uses already in Vedic and is continued unequivocally as a substantive in Assamese.

5 I.e., except for those languages that have loosened their SOV word order while retaining left-branching order at NP level, cf. §4.2.2 below.

and semantic equivalents to the ancient Indo-European examples. It should be noted in passing that we are dealing here with unextended appositions, that is, single-word appositions, since right displacement of extended appositions occurs quite commonly regardless of the word-order type, in keeping with the well-known tendency for heavy constituents to occur later in the clause.

In sum, OV word order $\wedge$ left-branching NP $\supset$ SPECIFIC + GENERIC (close unextended) APPOSITION.

The examples fall under five thematic rubrics:

A) REFERENT + GOD
B) REFERENT + KING/QUEEN
C) REFERENT + FATHER/MOTHER
D) REFERENT + MAN/WOMAN
E) REFERENT + ANIMAL/PLANT

Note that with the single exception of KING/QUEEN, each of the five categories of apposed nouns finds parallels in the inventory of Jacaltec classifiers, see Craig (1986: 266f.).

Ancient Indo-European languages	**Modern non-Indo-European languages**

A) REFERENT + GOD

Tocharian B	*yāmor*	***ñīkt-e***	Hungarian[6]	*Zeusz*	***isten***
	Karma:NOM	**god**-NOM		Zeus:NOM	**god**:NOM
		(B 496.5)			
Latin	*Mart-ī*	***de-ō***	Malayalam	*sōma*	***dēvan***
	Mars-DAT	**god**-DAT		Soma:NOM	**god**:NOM
(App. *Met.* 7.10.14; cf. *ThLL* 5.1.888 s.v. deus)					
Vedic	*savitā́*	***dev-ó***			
	Savitr̥:NOM	**god**-NOM			
		(RV 10.12.8d)			

6 Hungarian shows left-branching NP-level word order while allowing both SOV and SVO order at clause level, cf. §4.2.2 below.

B) REFERENT + KING/QUEEN

Tocharian A	*Siṃh-e*	***wäl***
	Siṃha-NOM	**king:NOM**
		(A 256a5)
Hittite	*Alalu-š*	***haššu-š***
	Alaluš-NOM	**king-NOM**
		(KUB 33.120 + i 8)
	Katešhaw-i	***haššuw-i***[7]
	Katešhawaš -DAT	**king-DAT**
		(KBo 25.122 iii 13)
Latin	*Amuli-us*	***rēx***
	Amulius-NOM	**king:NOM**
		(Fabius Pictor, FRH 1 F7c Beck&Walter)
Sanskrit	*Sóma*	***rā́jan***
	soma:VOC	**king:VOC**
		(RV 8.48.7c, 8a)
Hungarian	*Erzsébet*	***királynő***
	Elizabeth:NOM	**queen:NOM**
Malayalam	*Dāvīdə*	***rājāvə***
	David:NOM	**king:NOM**

C) REFERENT + FATHER/MOTHER

Tocharian A	*mahendradev-e*	***pācar***
	Mahendradeva-NOM	**father:NOM**
		(A 394 b2)
Luvian	*Tiwat-ī*	***dāt-ī*** [8]
	sun.god-DAT	**father-DAT**
		(KUB 35.107 Rs. iii 10, StBoT 30, 238)
Latin	*Mars*	***pater***
	Mars:NOM	**father:NOM**
		(Cato *Agr.* 141.2)
	terr-ai	***mātr-ī***
	earth-DAT	**mother-DAT**
		(CIL 1².995)
Hungarian	*Ábrahám*	***atya***
	Abraham:NOM	**father:NOM**
Malayalam	*abrāham*	***accan***
	Abraham:NOM	**father:NOM**
Quechua	*pacha*	***mama***
	earth	***mother***

Umbrian	ařmun-e	iuv-e	**patr-e**
	Ařsmo-DAT.SG	dius-DAT.SG	**father-DAT.SG**
	'to Jupiter Ařsmo'		
	(Rix 2002: IT IIb7)		

---

7 = ^{d}*Katešhawi*$_{i}$ LUGAL-*ui*.

8 = ^{d}UTU-*tī dātī*.

Oscan	*eukl-úí*	***pater-eí***
	Euklos-DAT	**father-DAT**
	(Rix 2002: TA A 25)	
Greek	Δη	-μήτηρ
	PIE **Deh$_2$*	***-meh$_2$tēr***
	Dā:NOM	**mother:NOM**
	'Demeter'	

The postposing of 'father' to an individual name is a remarkable syntactic archaism within Indo-European. This is confirmed by the name of the supreme deity of the Indo-European pantheon, Jupiter, literally 'Sky father', which displays exactly this ordering and can be crosslinguistically documented across the entire paradigm of inflected case forms, cf. for instance the vocative, nominative, and dative:

Cf.		SKY	FATHER			
					PIE	
***Vocative**	Latin	*Iu*	***-ppiter***	< *Iūpiter*	**d(í)i̯eu̯*	***ph́$_2$ter***
	Umbrian	iu	**pater**		oh Sky	**father**
	South Picene					
		toutiks di-	***pater****			
		gen. *toutikes di-*	***poteres***			
	Greek	Ζεῦ	**πάτερ**			
	Vedic	*dyàuṣ*	***pítar***			
Nominative	Latin	(**dius*	*piter)*		**d(i)i̯ḗu̯s*	***ph$_2$tḗr***
		diēs	*-piter*		Sky	**father**
	Greek	Ζεὺς	**πατήρ**			
	Vedic	*dyáuṣ*	***pitā́***			
Dative	Umbrian	*iuve*	***patre***		**diu̯éi̯*	*ph$_2$tréi̯*
	Luvian	*tiwatī*	***dātī***			

D) REFERENT + MAN/ WOMAN[9]

Hittite[10]	^{LÚ}*UR.GI$_7$-aš*	***pešn-aš*** [11]
	hunter-NOM	**man-NOM.SG**
	(KUB 12.126 i27, KUB 24.9 ii 27.50)	
	^{LÚ}*DAM.GÀR-š=a*	***pešn-iš*** [13]
	merchant-NOM=and	**man-NOM.PL**
	'(male) merchants'	
	(KUB 30.10 Rs 12-13)	
Tocharian A	*śākkiṣi-ñāñ*	***k$_u$lew-āñ***
	Śākya-NOM.PL	**woman-NOM.PL**
	(MSN 22 [III.2] b3f., Hackstein 2003: 149 n. 10)	

Tucano[12]	*semê*	***ɨmɨ***
	paca	**man**
	'male paca (a large rodent)'	
	semê	***numiô***
	paca	**woman**
	'female paca'	
	(Aikhenvald 2000:358 n.4)	
Turkish	*Fransız*	***kadın-lar-ı***
	French.people	**women-PL -POSS.3**[14]

Tocharian B	*kapyār-i*	***śrāy***	***klaiy-na***
	workers-NOM.PL	**adult.man:NOM.PL**	**woman-NOM.PL.F**
	'workers, men and women'		
			(SI B Toch./9.11[15])
Latin	*agn-um*	***mār-em***	
	lamb-ACC.SG	**man-ACC.SG**	
	'a male lamb'		
			(Fest. p. 204 Lindsay)

---

9 The juxtaposition of free lexemes denoting 'man/woman' is a typologically widespread strategy to express the sex of an animal, cf. Güldemann (1999: 69), Aikhenvald (2000: 358), Heine & Kuteva (2002: 209 [man > (4) male], 314f. [woman > (2) female]), and recently Patience Epps on Hup, a northwest Amazonian language of the Vaupés-Japura language family, see Epps (2007: 114 fn. 12). Cf. also §§8.1, 9.2 below. - With regard to Indo-European, note the Assamese definite non-human female classifier *-zɒni*, which is etymologically identifiable with Sanskrit *jániḥ* 'woman', e.g. Assamese *gai-zɒni* [cow-DEF.F.CL] 'the cow' (Goswami & Tamuli 2003: 417).

10 See CHD-P 326, sub *pešna-* e.

11 = ^{LÚ}*UR.GI$_7$-aš LÚ-aš.*

12 On the preferred OV constituency of the Tucanoan languages, see Dixon & Aikhenvald (1999: 224).

13 = ^{LÚ}*DAM.GÀR-š=a LÚ-iš.*

14 Formally, this is a head-marked genitive construction. Functionally, however, the given subtype is **not** possessive, but appositional.

15 Cf. Pinault (1998: 6), Schmidt (1999: 15f. fn.16). The *kapyāri* are monastery servants (Pinault 1994: 100f.), acting on behalf of the monastery together with their families, i.e. including both men and women.

Latin	*porc-um*	***fēmin-am***	
	pig-ACC.SG.M	**female-ACC.SG.F**	
	'the sow'		
			(Cato *Agr.* 134, 1)
Oscan	minat-eís	**ner-eís**	
	Minatus-GEN.SG	**man-GEN.SG**	
	'of the leader/hero Minatus'		
			(Rix 2002: Cp 25)
Homeric Greek	δμῳῇσι	**γυναιξί**	
	slaves.DAT.PL.F	**women.DAT.PL**	
			(Il. 6.323)
	βώτορ-ες	**ἄνδρ-ες**	
	herdsmen-NOM.PL	**men-NOM.PL**	
			(Od. 14.102, 17.200)

The positional characteristics of Homeric ἀνήρ 'man' are remarkable. Of the 30 occurrences of noun-noun appositional syntagms involving ἀνήρ, cases with postposed ἀνήρ strongly outnumber those with preposed ἀνήρ: as opposed to 22 cases of postposed ἀνήρ (Il. 1.594, 2.611, 6.315, 6.397, 9.477, 9.544, 10.477, 11.514, 11.687, 12.302, 13.390, 13.571, 16.495=532, 17.466, 23.845, Od. 8.584, 10.278, 14.102 = 17.200, 21.18, 24.253) we find only 8 cases with preposed ἀνήρ (Il. 11.92, 12.41, 12.170, 17.65, 21.574, Od. 9.91=96, 14.124). The tendency to postposing is too strong to be ascribable to metrical constraints only, but arguably is a faithful reflection of Homeric Greek grammar. In the framework of our theory, the postposing of ἀνήρ can be taken to be another manifestation of the original SOV constituency of Greek, which has already been claimed on other grounds, see Watkins (1976: 315-7), and Taylor (1994: 1f., 6-10, 18, 20, 33f.).

The same applies to Mycenean, which allows flexibility in clause-level word order (SOV, SVO) but retains left-branching word order in its NP-level parameters. Thus the Mycenean records attest to the positional schema of personal name plus title.[16]

---

16 Cf. Panagl (2006: 151). Examples are dat. sg. *At^hanai potnijai* 'to Athana, the mistress' (KN 5.52,1), *paro zowāi ereuteri* 'to Zowa, the inspector' (TH Av 100.4b), and *erita (h)ijereja* 'Erita, the priestess' (PY Ep 704.3). Furthermore, the type TOPONYM+CITY is likely to underlie Mycenean *Amnīson peda wastu* 'to the city of Amnison' (KN V (1) 114+158+7719 verso), if from **peda Amnīson wastu* by prosodic inversion of the proclitic preposition into phrase second position.

E) REFERENT + GENERIC (ANIMAL/ PLANT)

Homeric Greek	αἰετ-ὸς	**ὄρνι-ς**	
	eagle-NOM	**bird**-NOM	(Od. 19.548)
	χλουν-ῆν	**σῦ-ν**	
	boar-ACC.SG	**pig**-ACC.SG	(Il. 9.539)
Latin	*gladi-us*	***pisc-is***	
	sword-NOM	**fish**-NOM	(Plin. nat. 1.9.21)
	de Anthi-ā	***pisc-e***	
	about Anthias-ABL	**fish**-ABL	(Plin. *nat.* 9.69.180)
	apricul-um	***pisc-em***	
	hog-ACC	**fish**-ACC	(Enn. frg. var. 38)

Basque	*Arrano*	***hegazti**-a*
	eagle:NOM	**bird**:NOM-DET
Avar	*c‘c‘um*	***ħinč‘***
	eagle:NOM	**bird**:NOM
Avar	*ba‘ar*	***čču‘a***
	sturgeon:NOM	**fish**:NOM
Hungarian	*Anthias*	***hal***
	Anthias:NOM	**fish**:NOM

Latin	*ex*	*ole-ā*	***arbor-e***	
	from	olive-tree-ABL	**tree**-ABL	(Varro *rust.* 3.16.24)
	ex	*corn-ō*	***arbor-e***	
	from	cherry-tree-ABL	**tree**-ABL	(Fest. p. 33 Lindsay)
Tocharian B		*śarabh-e*	***luw-o***	
		śarabha-NOM	**animal**-NOM	(B358 a3)
		kurār	***lūw-o***	
		eagle.NOM	**animal**-NOM	(B88 b1)
	ce	*śarabh-eṃ*	***luw-a***	
	this	śarabha- OBL.SG.M	**animal**- OBL.SG.M	(B358 b2)

2.2. Head-initial word order and preposing of the generic noun

Given the demonstrated tendency for head-final languages to postpose (unextended) generic nouns, we now proceed to examine the reverse ordering, i.e.

VO ∧ right-branching NP ⊃ GENERIC + SPECIFIC (close unextended) APPOSITION.

2.2.1. Indo-European

Some Indo-European languages have already changed from SOV to SVO at the stage of their earliest attestation. A case in point is Old Church Slavonic, which is consistently head-initial. As expected, generic nouns are preposed to the referent, so that we find 'men that are fighters' or 'a human being which is god'.

Old Church Slavonic	***muž-i***	*borc-i*
	man-NOM.PL	fighter-NOM.PL
		(LLP II 269)
	člověk-ŭ	*bog-ŭ*
	human.being-NOM	god-NOM
		(LLP IV 879)

Likewise, most modern Indo-European languages, except for those belonging to the Indo-Iranian branch, have shifted to SVO clause-level word order. The default position of (unextended) close appositions in these languages is to have the generic term before the referent.

German	***Gott***	*Zeus*
	König	*Richard*
	Mutter	*Theresa*
	Mutter	*Erde*
	Vater	*Himmel*

2.2.2. Non-Indo-European

For the sake of completeness, I will also exemplify the preposing of close appositions for non-Indo-European languages with head-initial word-order configuration. Consider the following Biblical Hebrew examples:

Biblical	**’īš**	*kohēn*	**’iššāh**	*nəḇīʾāh*	***naʿărāh***	*ḇəṯūlāh*
Hebrew	**man**	priest	**woman**	prophetess	**girl**	virgin
(VSO)		(Lev 21,9)		(Judg 4,4)	(1 Kgs 1,2; Dt 22,23 +)	
	’īš	*sārīs*	**’iššāh**	*ʾalmānāh*		
	man	eunuch	**woman**	widow		
		(Jer 38,7)		(1 Kgs 7,14 11,26 +)		

Further non-IE languages exhibiting VO and APPOSITION-NOUN word order are: Zapotec (VSO [Black 2000: 45] & APP-N [Black 2000: 76], e.g., *lo x-mig Benito Jacinto* = face POSS-friend Benito Jacinto ‘to his (Benito’s) friend Jacinto’ [Black 2000: 149]); Guaraní (SVO [Gregores & Suárez 1967: 182] & APP-N, e.g., *yã Luisa* ‘Mrs Luisa’ [Gregores & Suárez 1967: 197]); Swahili (SVO [Ashton 1970: 44] & APP-N, e.g., *Bwana Ali* ‘Mr Ali’ [Ashton 1970: 86]); Malay (SVO [Sneddon 1996: 256] & APP-N [Sneddon 1996: 157-159], e.g., *Pak Sitepu* ‘Mr Sitepu’, Old Malay *dapunta hiyang* ‘lord god’ [Sneddon 2003: 38]); and Finnish (SVO & APP-N, e.g., *kuningatar Elisabeth* ‘Queen Elisabeth’, *herra/rouva professori Müller* ‘Mr/Mrs professor Müller’ [Petri Kallio, p.c.]).

3. More evidence for SOV and PROPER NOUN – COMMON NOUN order from ancient Indo-European languages: the case of Hittite, Tocharian, and Celtiberian

Important centerpieces of evidence are provided by two branches of Indo-European, Anatolian (Hittite) and Tocharian, which are otherwise known to preserve many archaisms of PIE date. Further test-cases are furnished by an other IE branch, Celtic, which is dominantly SVO but in which one isolated member attests to the same connection between SOV and N-APP order. That language is Celtiberian, which is particularly significant in light of its geographical isolation and preservation of archaisms lost elsewhere in Celtic. The Celtiberian SOV constituent order in fact deviates from the rest of Celtic. These facts, combined with the external evidence pointing to PIE as an SOV language, speak strongly in favor of Celtiberian SOV as a syntactic archaism. All three SOV languages, Hittite, Tocharian and Celtiberian, are important for our purposes since they require proper nouns to be followed by common nouns.

Given the importance of Anatolian and Tocharian, a fuller account of noun-noun appositional syntagms in these two branches seems called for.

Therefore, in what follows, I will briefly summarize the Hittite and Tocharian evidence. A section on Celtiberian will follow, which is necessarily shorter owing to the fragmentary attestation of this language.

3.1. Hittite: Postposed apposition

The basic constituent order of Hittite is SOV. In noun-noun appositional syntagms, the common noun is usually postposed to the proper noun. This rule, which is standard in Old Hittite, is relaxed somewhat in Middle and Neo Hittite, see Starke (1977: 156f.). There is a wealth of examples to be gleaned from the indices of proper and common names provided by many textual editions.[17] For titles, see for instance the index in Güterbock (1956 [10.4]: 122-127); for names of professions, Pecchioli-Daddi (1982); and for kinship terms, Hagenbuchner (1989). Regarding the postposition of common nouns, we find Hittite and Tocharian largely in agreement with each other. For the sake of illustration, I present the Hittite and Tocharian evidence under parallel rubrics, a comparison which yields many Hittite-Tocharian syntactic-semasiological (and in some cases even etymological) parallels, cf. Hittite *Mala=kan* ***ḫap-i*** 'Mala=PTCLE **river-LOC**' (KBo 12.100 Vs. 4) and Tocharian A *Gaṅk* ***āp-äṣ*** 'Ganges **river-ABL**' (A 45b2).

Rational beings

AB (A:PN + B:KING/GOD/PROFESSION)[18]

a) KING, POSITION

^{d}*Alalu-š*	***ḫaššu-š*** (*^{d}Alaluš LUGAL-uš*)	^{m}*Ḫani-š*	*BELU*
Alaluš-NOM	**king-NOM** (KUB 33.120 + i 8)	Haniš-NOM	**lord:NOM** (28 A iii 44, Güterbock 1956[10.3]: 96)
Labarn-aš	***ḫaššuw-aš***	^{m}*Ḫimuili-š=ma*	***GAL.GEŠTIN***
Labarnaš-GEN	**king-GEN** (KUB 57.63 II)	Himuiliš-NOM=PTCL	**commander:NOM** (28 i 11, Güterbock 1956[10.3]: 90)
^{d}*Katešḫaw-i*	***ḫaššuw-i***	^{m}*Ḫannutti-š*	*GAL ^{LÚ}IŠ*
Katešhawaš DAT	**king-DAT** (KBo 25.122 iii 13)	Hannuttiš-NOM	**marshal:NOM** (28 A i 12, Güterbock 1956[10.3]: 90)

17 Many thanks to Albertine Hagenbuchner for providing me with many references cited in this section. The given inventory, which is far from complete, is merely intended to illustrate the Hittite tendency for common nouns to be postposed to proper nouns.

18 Cf. *ḫaššu-* (HW² 3.439ff.), Güterbock (1956 [10.4]: 122-124).

b) GOD

ᵈKataḫḫa	***ᵈUTU-aš***		
Kataḫḫaš:NOM	**sun.deity**-GEN		
(CTH 633.B, KUB 51.57)			
ᵈḪalmaš[uiz] [19]	***šiu-š=miš***		
Ḫalmašuiz:NOM	**god**-NOM=**my**[20]		
(CTH 1.46-47)			

c) PROFESSION

ᵐZamna	***ᴸᵁ́DUG.GA₅.BUR***	*ᵐḪesni-š*	***ᴸᵁ́ŠÀ.TAM***
Zamnaš:NOM	**potter**:NOM	Ḫesniš-NOM	**financial.officer**:NOM
(A Vs. I, 17 62, Souček [1959: 12, 15])		(KUB 13.33 ii 5, StBoT 4.34)	
ᵐḪutarli	***ᴸᵁ́SANGA***	*ᵐŠaḫli-š*	***ᴸᵁ́DAM.GÀR***
Ḫutarliš:NOM	**priest**:NOM	Šaḫliš-NOM	**merchant**:NOM
(KUB 38.37 Rs. iii 8, StBot 4.56)		(KUB 13.34 i 13, StBoT 4.38)	

AC (A:PN + C:KINSHIP TERM, GENDER/AGE)[21]

ᵐZidant-an	***att-a(n)=šan***	*ᵐAlamuw-aš=a*	***DUMU.NITA***
Zidantaš-ACC	**father**-ACC=**his**	Alamuwaš-NOM=and	**boy**:NOM
'his father Zidantaš'		'and the boy Alamuwaš'	
(CTH 19, I 68, THeth. 11.24; HW² I 543f. s.v. *atta-*)		(KUB 13.35 iii 43, StBoT 4.12)	
ᵐPitḫan-aš	***att-aš=maš*** *appan*		
Pitḫanaš-GEN.SG	**father**-GEN.SG.=**my** after		
'after my father Pitḫanaš'			
(CTH 1, Vs. 30, StBoT 18.12)			

19 Restoration after Singer (1995: 347).

20 Note that the postposing of the extended noun *šiuš=**miš*** cannot be the result of "heavy constituency", since the suffixation of pronominal clitics to a noun does not generate heaviness in terms of the "heaviness to the right" principle. Thus, in Hittite (SOV), GEN-N order remains unchanged regardless of whether the genitive is extended by a clitic possessive-pronoun suffix or not, e.g.: *atta(š-)**šaš** piri (É-ri)* [father-her house-in] 'in the house of her father' (Hoffner 1997: 36, §27, J 9). Likewise, in Biblical Hebrew (VSO) the suffixation of a possessive-pronoun suffix to a common noun does not cause it to be postposed to a following proper noun: *'aḇḏə-**ḵā** yaʿăqoḇ* [servant-your Jacob] 'your servant Jacob' (Gn. 32.5) *bin-**ḵā** yōsēp̱* [son-your Joseph] 'your son Joseph' (Gn. 45.9) ***'āḥ-ī*** *ḇinyāmīn* [brother-my Benjamin] 'my brother Benjamin' (Gn. 45.12).

21 Cf. *atta-* (HW² I 541ff.), Hagenbuchner 1989, Güterbock (1956[10.4]: 122-124).

AD (A:PN + D:GENERAL TERM OF ADDRESS)

^{d}U	***išḫāš=miš*** [22]	*^{d}UTU^{si}*	*BELI=^{YA}*
weather.god	**lord=my**	sun.god	**lord=my**
	(KBo 43.52 iv 14)		(CTH 200, ABoT 60 Vs. 20-22)

SPECIFIC + GENERIC

Šerri Ḫurri	GUD$^{ḪI.A}$-*ri*
Šerriš:NOM [and] Hurriš:NOM	**bulls:NOM**

(KBo. 17.86 i 4, KBo. 20.119 vi 26)

Inanimate beings

The basic specific-generic order pertains not only to human beings but also to inanimate items:

TOPONYM + CITY

^{URU}Iyaruwad-aš	***ḫappir-aš*** [23]
Iyaruwadaš-NOM	**city**-NOM

(KBo 3.3 I 14)

This type is sporadically found in Latin, e.g., *Satricum* ***urbem*** (Liv. 6.33,4). Many more examples are listed in the *Hethitisches Wörterbuch* (HW^{2} 3.237f., s.v. *ḫappira-*); cf. Quechua (OV) *La Paz* ***llaxta*** 'La Paz, city'.

HYDRONYM + RIVER

Mala=kan	***ḫap-i***
Malaš=PTCL	**river**-LOC

'in the river Mala'

(KBo 12.100 Vs. 4, cf. HW^{2} 3.201 sub *ḫapa-* II.4da)

3.2. Tocharian: Postposed apposition

The unmarked constituent order of Tocharian is SOV (see the references cited in Hackstein 2003: 134). Within noun-noun appositional syntagms, the default position of the appositional common noun is **after** the proper noun. A list of examples is provided in Sieg, Siegling & Schulze

22 = *^{d}U EN-YA.*

23 = *^{URU}Iyaruwadaš URU-aš.*

(1931: 209-217) and Hackstein (2003: 134-137). A subrule (to be dealt with below in a somewhat broader context, see §4.2.1) stipulates that the common noun may be preposed if it is used as a term of address and consequently occurs in stressed, highlighted position (cf. Sieg, Siegling & Schulze 1931: 209 fn. 2). Thus, the Tocharian B vocative *saswa* 'sir' is almost always preposed, e.g., B83,6 ***saswa*** *appakka* 'oh sir father', BH149.82b2 *saswa pācer* 'oh sir father', B93 a2 ***säswemntse*** *(ara)ṇemiñ lānte* 'of sir Araṇemi, the king', likewise A101b4 ***nātäk*** *nande* 'oh sir Nanda' and MSN 15[I.7] a2 ***pracar*** *Purṇabhadre* 'oh brother Pūrṇabhadra' (as against non-vocative *Ajiteṃ* ***pracräṣṣ*** 'from brother Ajita' MSN 14[II.5]b7).

Rational beings

AB (PN + KING, GOD, PROFESSION)

a) KING, POSITION

Virupākṣ-es	***lānt***
Virūpākṣa-GEN	**king**:GEN
	(Toch. MSN 6 [II.8] a3)

Araṇemi-ñ	***lānt-e***
Araṇemi-GEN	**king**-GEN
	(Toch. B 77.4)

Prasenaji-ṃ	***lānt***
Prasenaji-OBL	**king**:OBL
	(Toch. A 433b5)

Subhāṣitagawesi-ṃ	***lānt***
Subhāṣitagawesi-OBL	**king**:OBL
	(Toch. B 99a2)

Ikṣvākṣu-ñ	***lāṃś***
Ikṣvākṣu-NOM.PL	**king**:NOM.PL
	(Toch. A 101a4)

Vidyādhare-ñ	***lāś***
Vidyādhare-NOM.PL	**king**:NOM.PL
	(Toch. A 317b8)

Gautami-ṃ	***latsā-c***
Gautami-OBL	**queen**:OBL-ALL
	(Toch. A MSN 25 [III.6] b6)

b) GOD

humā-ṃ	***ñäkteṃñā-ṃ***
Huma-OBL	**goddess**-OBL
	(Toch. A 201a2)

Śākyamuni-ṃ	***ptāñkt-ac***
Śākyamuni-OBL	**Buddha.god**:OBL-ALL
	(Toch. A 23a2)

c) PROFESSION

Vardhane-ṃ	***wapānts-ai***	*Araṇemi*	***werpiśkatsts-e***
Vardhana-OBL	**weaver-OBL**	Araṇemi:NOM	**gardener-NOM**
	(Toch. B375b2)		(Toch. B 91 a3, b2, 5, B 92 a4)
Bṛhadyuti-ṃ	***kuntistsekā-n-ac***	*Drayośvare*	***käryorttau***
Bṛhadyuti-OBL	**potter-OBL-ALL**	Drayośvara: NOM	**merchant:NOM**
	(Toch. A 19b5f.)		(Toch. B 89 b5)
Rudhramukhe-ṃ	***purohite-ṃ***		
Rudhramukha-OBL	**priest-OBL**		
	(Toch. B 88 b6)		

AC (PN + KINSHIP, GENDER, GENDER/AGE), cf. above p. 12f. §2.1C.

Brahmāyu	***pācar***	*Ajite-ṃ*	***pracr-äṣṣ***
Brahmāyu:NOM	**father:NOM**	Ajita-OBL	**brother:OBL-ABL**
	(A 258b5, Pinault 2004: 74)		(A MSN 14[II.5]b7)
Brahmāvati	***mācr-ac***	*Śuke-ṃ*	***kālśke-ṃ***
Brahmāvati:OBL	**mother:OBL-ALL**	Śuka-OBL	**boy-OBL**
	(Toch. A 258b4, Pinault 2004: 74)		(Toch. B H149add 63/59b6)

AD (PN + GENERAL TERM OF ADDRESS)

Nande	***nātäk***
Nande:NOM	**sir:NOM**
	(Toch. A 99b6)

SPECIFIC + GENERIC

Śarabh-e	***luw-o***	*Aineye-ntse*	***lwā-ntse***
Śarabha-NOM	**animal-NOM**	Aineya-GEN	**animal-GEN**
	(Toch. B 358 a3)		(Toch. B 74a4)

Inanimate beings

TOPONYM + CITY

Bārāṇaṣ	***riy-äṣ***
Vārāṇasī:OBL	**city:OBL-ABL**
	(Toch. A MSN 1 [I.10]a1f.)

HYDRONYM + RIVER

Gaṅk	***āp-äṣ***
Ganges:OBL	**river:OBL-ABL**

'from the river of Ganges'

(Toch. A 45b2)

3.3. Celtiberian: Postposed apposition

The word order of Celtiberian is strictly SOV (Eska 1989: 176, 1994[95]: 17f.). Although the fragmentary nature of the Celtiberian linguistic corpus does not allow us to compile a collection of examples as rich as those given above for Hittite and Tocharian, the evidence points unequivocally to a strict postposing of titles in Celtiberian. The canonical Celtiberian onomastic formula consistently attests to a structure in which a tripartite naming formula (proper name + gen. pl. of the nomen gentile + gen. sg. of patronym) is followed by a common noun (the title, marked by boldface type in the following examples). Particularly instructive in this respect is the Botorrita inscription (face B) composed of 14 names, e.g. *luPoś CouneśiCum melmunoś* ***bintiś***, with the title *bintiś* lit. 'binder', i.e., the one in charge of securing the treaty.[24] Closer inspection of the remaining corpus reveals additional examples, such as the grave inscription K.16.1 *tirtanos abulokum letontunoś kentiś* ***belikioś*** 'Tirtanos, of the Abulokoi, Letontu's son, **the Belikian**' or the *tessera hospitalis* K.0.11 ... *bistiroś lastiko* ***ueizoś*** 'Bistiros, Lastiko's [son], **witness**' (David Stifter, p.c.).

4. The syntax of simple apposition and word-order type

4.1. Greenberg's Universal 23

The positional characteristics of nominal apposition were discussed by Greenberg (1966: 89-90, 112), who proposed drawing a correlation between the appositional noun (common noun) and the dependent genitive.[25] According to Greenberg's Universal 23, the positional characteristics of head and apposed noun ought to coincide with those of governing noun and dependent genitive: "If in apposition the proper noun usually precedes the common noun, then the language is one in which the governing noun precedes the genitive. With much better than chance frequency, if the common noun usually precedes the proper noun, the dependent genitive precedes its governing noun" (Greenberg 1966: 89f.). The prediction is that the apposition (more precisely, the apposed common noun) will be

---

24 Cf. Eska (1989: 126f.), Motta (1993: 707).

25 However, Greenberg (1966: 89) expresses some reservation: "My data here are incomplete because grammars often make no statement on the subject."

postposed if the genitive is postposed, and preposed if the genitive is preposed. Schematically:

(i) Universal 23a	PROPER NOUN – **COMMON NOUN (AP)**	
	NOUN – **GENITIVE**	(= right-branching NP structure)
Universal 23b	**COMMON NOUN (AP)** – PROPER NOUN	
	GENITIVE – NOUN	(= left-branching NP structure)

Both of Greenberg's claims, however, are counterexemplified by the material presented here as well as in Hackstein (2003). The evidence strongly suggests that, contrary to Greenberg's Universal 23, the ordering of proper and common noun cannot be aligned with that of noun and dependent genitive. On the contrary, the two constructions (i.e., N–AP and N–GEN) present the exact mirror image of each other; see the boldfaced constituents in the following scheme:

(ii)	PROPER NOUN – **COMMON NOUN (AP)**
	GENITIVE – NOUN (= left-branching NP structure)
	COMMON NOUN (AP)– PROPER NOUN
	NOUN– **GENITIVE** (= right-branching NP structure)

In addition, Greenberg's approach is undermined by the fact that Universal 23 is not clearly supported even by the languages, on which he bases his claims (Greenberg 1996: 106 n. 19). These languages are, for Universal 23a, Greek, Guaraní, Italian, Malay, Serbian, Swahili, Thai, Welsh, Zapotec; and for Universal 23b, Basque, Burmese, Burushaski, Finnish, Japanese, Norwegian, Nubian, Turkish. Of the languages with COMMON NOUN (AP)-PROPER NOUN order adduced in support of Universal 23b, Greek, Italian, Serbian, Swahili and Zapotec do not comply with the predicted GEN-N order. Rather, contrary to Universal 23b and in accordance with (ii) above, these languages either consistently or optionally show N-GEN order. Similarly, of the languages with PROPER NOUN-COMMON NOUN (AP) order, Basque, Burushaski, Japanese, and Turkish – contrary to Greenberg's claim – do not exhibit N-GEN order but GEN-N order, again in accordance with the correlation drawn in (ii) above. Furthermore, Norwegian does not exhibit the PROPER NOUN-COMMON NOUN order, cf. *konge Harald* 'king Harald'.

Given the revision of Greenberg's Universal 23 presented in (ii) above, and the recognition of PROPER NOUN-COMMON NOUN order as inherently left-branching (and COMMON NOUN–PROPER NOUN order as inherently right-branching), a number of apparent language-specific exceptions to Greenberg's correlation turn out to be consistent with the expected branching direction. An example is Heine & Reh's (1984: 246) observation that the West African Mande languages, which have dominant SOV order[26], contradict Greenberg's Universal 23: "In Mande languages, the proper noun precedes the common noun, but the governing noun always follows its dependent genitive."

Màlí nyàmanɛ
Mali nation:DEF
'the state of Mali'

Heine & Reh (1984:247) suggest that this word-order type might be related to a shift from earlier SVO syntax to SOV syntax. In light of the evidence presented in this monograph, however, the given positional type need not constitute a remnant of SVO syntax, but is fully consistent with SOV syntax.

4.2. Evidence against N-AP & SOV, subrules and diachronic change

Regarding the claim that the postposing of unextended close apposition (N-AP) is consistent with SOV syntax, several reservations must be made.

First, it must emphasized that the proposed correlation between N-AP word order and SOV syntax is essentially based on data from ancient Indo-European languages; the scant data adduced here from non-Indo-European languages is far from being representative of all language families. Nevertheless, if there is empirical evidence from ancient Indo-European and some non-Indo-European languages for an N-AP ordering driven by semantic dependency relations like hyponymity and hyperonymity, then the underlying ordering principle has a good chance of being based on universal semantic relations that are independent of language-specific structures and therefore likely to recur cross-linguistically. Further typological research is clearly necessary.

Second, alongside semantic-based ordering there are also other competing mechanisms blurring the N-AP & SOV correlation. These mechanisms can be either synchronic or diachronic.

---

[26] Mande is not a typical SOV language type, however. A more precise characterization of its constituent structure would be "S-**Aux**-O-V-**Other**" (O. Gensler, p.c.).

Synchronically and from a purely syntactic point of view, there is linguistic evidence (for instance from Latin) to suggest that in binomial appositional pairs both nouns are eligible morphosyntactic heads, as can be seen from the fact that both may project morphological information on to dependent or coreferential nouns. If the syntactic status of N and AP is the same, the ordering of N and AP ought in principle to be syntactically free. If, however, a language gives preference to a semantically driven order of apposition, then the hyperonymic apposition will act as the semantic and morphosyntactic head (as in ancient Indo-European languages and in Modern German) and the appositional word order will comply with the semantic branching direction.

Other mechanisms that can reverse the expected N-AP & SOV correlation involve the existence of synchronic subrules (see §4.2.1. on highlighting), and diachronic mechanisms like ongoing or accomplished word-order changes (§4.2.2.) and morphosyntactic changes (see §4.2.3. on adjectival conversion of AP and syntactic analogy).

4.2.1. Highlighting

As regards sub-rules, one such rule can be established beyond any doubt. SOV languages allow the PROPER NOUN-COMMON NOUN order to be inverted if the common noun is to be highlighted. Such left-dislocation of otherwise postposed titles as a highlighting device can be observed in a number of languages.

In the third volume of his *Vergleichende Syntax* (1900:199), Delbrück noted that the Vedic tendency to prepose the title *rā́jā* 'king' is especially strong with the god Varuṇa, and that in this case the emphatic preposing is well accounted for by Varuṇa's being the supreme god in the Vedic pantheon.

In Latin, toponymic appositions such as *urbs, oppidum* 'city' are postposed (e.g., Latin *Satricum urbs*); but in the case of Rome, the capital city, the toponym is more often preposed: *urbs Roma*, cf. Kühner & Stegmann (1955: 604): "Immer in guter Prosa *urbs Roma*" and Leumann, Hofmann & Szantyr (1972: 409).

In Tocharian, it is normal for titles such as Tocharian A *nātäk* 'sir' to be postposed to an accompanying proper name. Nevertheless, an inversion of this order and preposing of the title are found in those vocatives where the title is communicatively particularly important, e.g. vocative *nātäk nande* 'sir Nanda', see above §3.2.

The tendency described accords well with Givón's more general prediction (2001: 278) that "L-dislocating a definite referent (80b) signals its importance."

4.2.2. Word-order change

Other inconsistencies, such as co-occurrence in the same language of left-branching NPs alongside basic SVO order, or right-branching NPs alongside basic SOV order, often find a diachronic explanation. Diachronic syntactic change may change the NP-level word order from left-branching to right-branching while leaving the clause-level order (SOV) intact. An example is Modern Persian, which is SOV at the clause level (Lass 2000:180-181) yet preposes the apposition.

Conversely, clause-level word order may be loosened from strict SOV to flexible SVO (e.g. Hungarian, Basque)[27] or VSO (e.g. Lycian), while leaving the left-branching NP-level word order intact. Thus Hungarian shows left-branching NP-level word order including postposed appositions; at the same time, its clause-level word order is much less constrained, permitting SVO word order as well, cf. Kiss (1987:21). Similarly, Lycian, an ancient IE language of the Anatolian branch, shows a left-branching NP structure including postposed appositions, e.g. *padrñma* ***kumaza*** 'Padrñma **the priest**' (TL 49, Neumann 1993: 35), *wataprddata* ***χssadrapa*** 'Wataprddata **the Satrap**' (TL 40 d1, Neumann 1982: 149). At the same time, the Proto-Anatolian SOV order at the clause level has changed to Lycian VSO.

4.2.3. Adjectival conversion of AP and syntactic analogy

Several ancient Indo-European languages attest to the adjectival zero conversion of appositional nouns, whereby the adjectivally converted postposed noun moves into the prenominal adjectival slot (see §9.2.2.1.2.). This leftward movement of the adjectivized AP is furthered by syntactic analogy and alignment with other left-branching NP types of the structure modifier-plus-head, e.g. Gen-N.

---

27 King & Elordi (1996: 201), Trask (1997: 109).

5. The internal dependency structure of NPs involving close apposition: head-final, head-initial or double-headed?

It is striking that not much work has been invested so far in correlating appositional syntax and word order, but perhaps this is for a good reason. In fact, however manifest this particular correlation may seem, it turns out to be very difficult to account for.

We have seen that postposing of close apposition is preferred in head-final languages. The most natural way to explain this would be to say that the appositional construction is itself a head-dependent structure, and that the closely apposed noun – the generic nominal – is the head of the construction. This, however, is an issue on which opinions have differed greatly. Altogether four standpoints are possible in analyzing an NP like 'king Richard': a) 'king' is the head, b) 'Richard' is the head, c) both 'king' and 'Richard' are the head, [28] d) with regard to the Australian generic-specific construction, typologists have suggested that either constitutent, the generic or the specific noun, can function as head (cf. Dixon 2002: 455), in which case "the question of syntactic headship in noun phrases which consist of a noun classifier and a noun has to be established on a language-specific basis" (Aikhenvald 2000: 90).

In addition, numerous tests have been proposed, which however fail to yield a consistent picture. Some such tests "prove" the transformational equivalence of the apposition with an attribute, supporting the canonical belief that the apposition is a kind of attribute.[29] For instance, it is possible to transform the apposition into a relative clause, or to replace it by attributive pronouns/adjectives, cf. Heberlein (1996: 349f.). One must bear in mind, however, that transformational equivalence does not automatically imply identity of underlying structure or representation. In addition, there is evidence for the reverse analysis, for other syntactic tests point in the opposite direction, identifying the close apposition as the head of the NP. Thus in some languages, appositions are treated like heads in

---

28 Cf. Lehmann (1988: 181), Heberlein (1996: 343, 351, 353), and Lawrenz (1993: 134): "es handelt sich um semantisch und syntaktisch 'gleichgewichtige' und 'nebengeordnete' Konstituenten."

29 Cf. for instance Schwyzer (1947:9 n. 2) on the affinity of apposition, attribute and predicate, Seiler (1960: 36), Heberlein (1996: 343 fn. 4), Pinault (1997a: 129), and Lühr (1996: 89): "Die Apposition ist ein substantivisches Attribut, das im allgemeinen im gleichen Kasus steht wie das Bezugswort (...). Durch Umformung der nominalen Fügung in einen Satz wird die Apposition zur Prädikatsnomen-Ergänzung."

that they determine the gender of a coreferential relative pronoun, thus meeting one of the criteria defining the notion of a head, cf. Primus (2001: 857): "the head is the determining category in terms of case government or other valency related phenomena in which one element determines the presence, syntactic or semantic function of another element." If in a juxtaposition of proper noun and common noun the two differ as to their gender, it is more often the common noun that determines the gender of coreferential pronouns rather than the proper noun.[30] Cf. the Latin examples below, in which the appositional common nouns *flumen/urbs* and not the juxtaposed proper nouns trigger gender concord:

flumen[N]	*Axonam*[F],	***quod***[N] *est in extremis Remorum finibus.*
river.ACC.SG.N	Axona.ACC.SG.F	**REL.NOM.SG.N** be.PRS.3.SG PRP extreme.ABL.PL border.ABL.PL

"**the river** Axona, **which** is situated in the border area of the Remi" (Caes. *BG* 2.5,4)

Satricum[N]	***urbem***[F],	***quae***[F] *receptaculum fuerat.*
Satricum.ACC.SG.N	**city.ACC.SG.F**	**REL.NOM.SG.F** refuge.NOM.SG.N be.PRT.3SG.ACT

"Satricum, **the city, which** has been their refuge" (Liv. 6.33,4)

The priority of the common noun over the proper noun can be observed in modern Indo-European languages too. To take an example, German city names, such as *Krefeld*, trigger neuter concord in coreferential possessive pronouns. However, when juxtaposed to a feminine common noun like *Stadt* 'city', it is the common noun 'city' and not the proper noun that controls the gender of coreferential possessives.

Krefeld[N]	*kümmert sich um*	***seine***[N] *Bürger.*
Krefeld.NOM.SG.N	care.PRS.3.SG REFL PRP	**POSS.N.ACC.PL** citizen.ACC.PL

"Krefeld cares for its citizens."

[30] Cf. for Latin Kühner & Stegmann (1955:43f.), Heberlein (1996: 348, 350), and for German Lawrenz (1993: 45-47).

Die Stadt[F]	*Krefeld*[N]	*kümmert sich um*	***ihre***[F] *Bürger.*
ART.NOM.SG.F **city**.NOM.SG.F	Krefeld.NOM.SG.N	care.PRS.3.SG REFL PRP	POSS.F.ACC.PL citizen.ACC.PL

"The city of Krefeld cares for its citizens."

The same observation holds for the feminine noun *Eiche* 'oak' and its masculine generic hyperonym Baum 'tree'.

Die Eiche[F]	*verliert*	***ihre***[F] *Blätter.*
ART.NOM.SG.F **oak**.NOM.SG.F	lose.PRS.3.SG	POSS.F.ACC.PL leaf.ACC.PL

"The oak loses its leaves."

Der Baum[M]	*Eiche*	*verliert*	***seine***[M] *Blätter.*
ART.NOM.SG.M **tree.** NOM.SG.M	oak.NOM.SG.F	lose.PRS.3.SG	POSS.M.ACC.PL leaf.ACC.PL

"The oak tree loses its leaves."

5.1. Semantic subordination and hyponymity/hyperonymity

Given the indeterminacy of the syntactic tests described above, it seems advisable to ignore such aprioristic methods for the moment, and to start anew from the empirical and descriptive fact that OV syntax usually implies NOUN-APPOSITION word order and conversely VO syntax APPOSITION-NOUN word order. As has been documented above, there is a widespread tendency for the position of the generic noun to be connected with the Consistent Head Serialization Principle: NOUN-APPOSITION order correlates with OV order, and APPOSITION-NOUN order correlates with VO order. Nonetheless, these descriptive facts are not by themselves an explanation. Taking NOUN-APPOSITION and OV word order as examples, it seems as though the NOUN-APPOSITION syntax is not explained but rather contradicted by OV word order, for the following reason. If we analyse the apposition as a kind of attribute, as most linguists would, then the NOUN-APPOSITION syntax would be reformulated as core information plus accessory information, i.e., as NOUN-ATTRIBUTE or HEAD-MODIFIER structure—the exact opposite of the head-final MODIFIER-HEAD structure that ought to go along with OV syntax.

Fortunately, it is possible to resolve this problem and demonstrate that the ordering of specific noun and generic apposition can indeed be reconciled with a left- and right-branching dependency structure. In what follows I will try to show that the key to the problem is to be sought in the semantic relationship of the juxtaposed units. More specifically, we will envision the relationship of specific noun plus generic apposition as one of **semantic subordination:** the linearly first noun is semantically subordinated to the second, apposed noun. Consider the two sets of examples given below, showing the ordering typical for OV languages. In each case the corresponding items in the left and right columns are to be taken together, as jointly forming an ordered constituent:

Semantic Scope	(+) more specific	(-) less specific
A1	*trout*	FISH
A2	*copper*	METAL
B1	*Richard*	KING
B2	*Mars*	GOD
	Hyponym	Hyperonym

For each pair, the left and right items differ from each other with regard to their semantic scope. Moving from right to left, i.e., from the the second unit to the first unit, we proceed from a less specific to a more specific kind of information. The more general term 'fish' is narrowed down by 'trout', and the more general term 'metal' by 'copper'. Similarly, the titles 'king' and 'god' identify a social class, whereas the proper name identifies an individual member of that class. In each case, we find a class-versus-member relationship between the second and the first unit. Semantically, the first unit can be analyzed as a hyponym, and the second unit as its hyperonym.

Note that there is a subtle semantic difference between rubric A and rubric B. In the case of rubric A the semantic inclusion is logically obligatory: every trout is a fish, whereas in the case of rubric B) the inclusion is logically optional: not every person called Richard is a king. To capture this difference, it has been suggested that such optional hyponyms of kind B be called **pseudo-hyponyms**, see Cruse (1975: 30). But aside from this subtle difference, the semantic relationship of the two units may be described as that of meaning inclusion (member-class relationship), with the apposition functioning as a hyperonym and the first unit functioning as a hyponym.

Now the terms hyponym and hyperonym already involve, by definition, a semantic dependency relationship: the hyperonym is semantically superordinated, and the hyponym semantically subordinated. In OV languages, the typical example would be "trout – FISH". Here, the disambiguation of the semantic content proceeds from right to left, from less specific to more specific information or from general information to a more particular kind of information.

6. Semantic chaining: Leftward relocation of hyponyms in OV languages

As I have argued elsewhere (Hackstein 2003: 143ff.), the idea of semantically governed dependency structures is further supported by the phenomenon of left-relocation of hyponyms in head-final languages. It can be shown that as a rule, OV languages tend to place hyponyms to the left of their relative hyperonyms.[31] A hyponym like *trout* is correspondingly placed to the left of its relative hyperonym *fish*. But the given hyperonym, here *fish*, can itself be a hyponym with respect to a still more general noun such as *animal*; this means that the hyperonym *fish* now becomes a hyponym, and is accordingly relocated to the left of a further superordinate semantic hyperonym *animal*.

Hyponymity and hyperonymity are relative concepts (Hackstein 2003: 143). Therefore, in a binomial syntagm, the transformation of a relative hyperonym into a relative hyponym accords with its relocation from final NP position to initial NP position.

---

31 I use the term left(ward) relocation to avoid any confusion with the well-established term "left dislocation". Unlike left dislocation, which designates movement out of the normal position, left relocation is a static, purely descriptive term. Based on the iterative right-to-left hyponymic ordering of appositions, it denotes the phenomenon whereby one and the same noun, which occurs on the right of the NP if hyperonymic, is relocated to the left of the NP if hyponymic.

FIGURE 1. *Hyponymity and Hyperonymity as relative concepts*

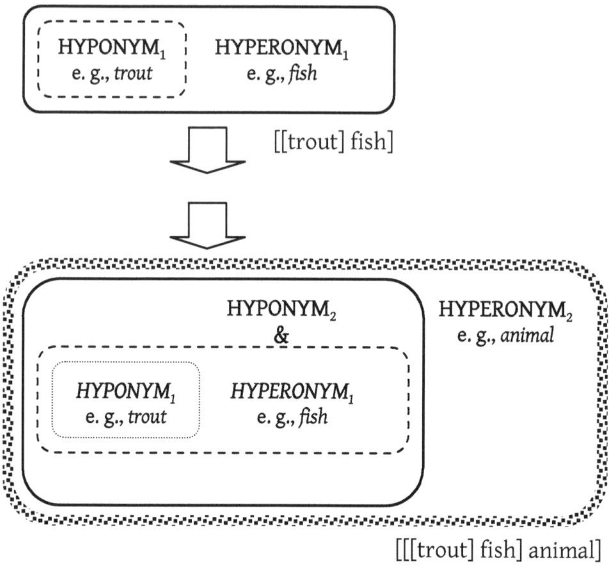

In Hackstein (2003: 147), I demonstrated this for a schema/grid of four semantic types of NPs, which can combine linearly to form noun-noun appositional phrases:

A (proper names)
B (appositions signifying social status, profession)
C (kinship terms, gender/age)
D (general terms of address).

Left-branching NP structures prefer the ordering A+B+C+D. The guiding principle behind this ordering is semantic dependency and subordination. Breaking the chain A+B+C+D down into three pairs, i.e., A+B, B+C, and C+D, we see that each of these involves a hyponym plus hyperonym relationship, yielding a hierarchically structured order, ascending from the more specific to the more general (Hackstein 2003: 141-143, 147-148), schematically:
A (hyponym^{B}) + B (hyperonym^{A} & hyponym^{C}) + C (hyperonym^{B} & hyponym^{D}) + D (hyperonym^{C}).
This notation is to be read "A is a hyponym of B, plus B, which is a hyperonym of A and a hyponym of C, plus C, which is a hyperonym of B and a hyponym of D, plus D, which is a hyperonym of C."

In sum, within a left-branching NP structure:

A is relocated to the left by B, C, D (A←B←C←D)
B is relocated to the left by C, D (B←C←D)
C is relocated to the left by D (C←D).

FIGURE 2. *Leftward relocation of hyponyms*

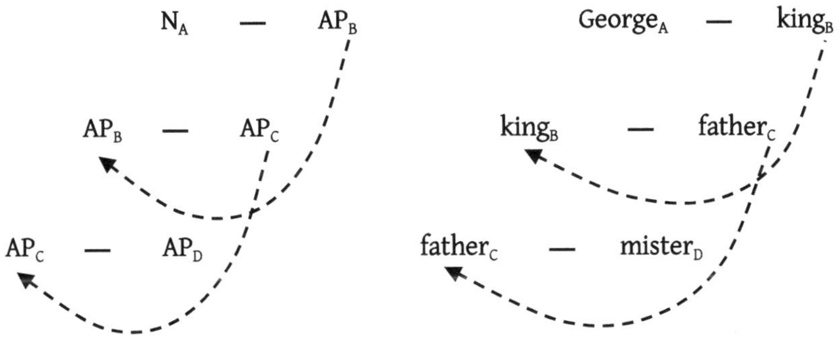

All of these relocation types can be exemplified for both Indo-European and non-Indo-European languages. Within ancient Indo-European, a wealth of examples is offered by Hittite and Tocharian. In accordance with the above principles, the following semantic chaining obtains for 'king' (Hittite *haššuš*, Tocharian B *walo*), 'god' (Hittite *šiuš*/^{d}UTU, Tocharian B *ñakte*), 'father' (Hittite *attaš*, Tocharian B *pācer*) and 'master/mister' (Hittite *išhāš*, Tocharian *käṣṣi*):

	A	← B king, god	← C father	← D master/mister
Hittite	PN	*haššuš, šiuš*/^{d}UTU	*attaš, pešnaš*	*išhāš*
Tocharian A&B	PN	*walo, ñakte*	*pācer, āl*	*käṣṣi*
Greek	PN	βασιλεύς	πατήρ, ἀνήρ	

[PN = personal name; A← B is to be read "A is relocated to the left by B."]

In Homeric Greek, the term for 'king', βασιλεύς, is frequently postposed. However, it is displaced to the left if it cooccurs with the more general generic noun ἀνήρ 'man'.

A ← B (A:PN + B:KING, GOD, PROFESSION)
B ← C (B:KING, GOD, PROFESSION + C:KINSHIP TERM, GENDER/AGE)

Ancient Greek	AB	Ῥῆσος	**βασιλεύς**
		Rhesos **king**	
			(Il. 10.435)
	BC	βασιλῆ-ι [γὰρ] **ἄνδρ-ι**[32]	
		king-DAT [PTCL] **man-DAT**	
			(Il. 3.170)

In Hittite, the term for 'king', *haššuš*, tends to be postposed; but again 'king' is relocated to the left when cooccurring with a general kinship term such as 'father'.

Hittite	AB	*Katešhaw-i*	***haššuw-i***
		Katešhawa-DAT	**king-DAT**
			(KBo 25.122 iii 13)
	BC	*haššu-i*	***att-i=mi***[33]
		king-DAT	**father-DAT=my**
			(KUB 26.35,4, HW 1^2.544, s.v. *atta-*)

Likewise, it is normal for Hittite titles of professions to follow the proper name. However, they too are relocated to the left by the generic noun *pešnaš* 'man'.

Hittite	AB	^{m}*Šaḫliš*	^{LÚ}***DAM.GÀR***
		Šaḫliš	**merchant**
			(KUB 13.34 i 13, StBoT 4.38)
	BC	^{LÚ}*UR.*GI_7*-aš*	***pešnaš***
		hunter	**man**
			(KUB 12.126 i27, KUB 24.9 ii 27.50)

The ordering type BC is pervasive in Hittite and can be further exemplified:

---

[32] It is true that here the reverse order ἄνδρι [γὰρ] βασιλῆι would be metrically impossible in any case. Yet the attested order βασιλῆι [γὰρ] ἄνδρι stands a good chance of being the original, metrically unconstrained order in light of the general tendency for ἀνήρ to occur after the noun it classifies, see La Roche (1893: 201f.).

[33] = LUGAL-*i* ***att-i=mi***. cf. Luvian *Tiwat-ī* ***dāt-ī*** = sun.god-DAT **father-DAT** (KUB 35.Rs. iii 10).

Hittite	BC	^{D}UTU$^{-ši}$	*ABI=YA*
		sun.god:VOC=my	**father:VOC=my**
			(text no. 213, Hagenbuchner 1989: 314)
	BC	*šiun-eš*	***pišen-eš***[34]
		god-NOM.PL	**men-NOM.PL**
		'the gods, (i.e.,) the males'[35]	
			(CHD-P 327, sub *pešna-* i)

In the same vein, a B-item such as *šiuš* (=^{D}UTU-*uš*) 'god' is postposed except when cooccurring with a D-item like the more general title *išḫā-* 'lord', in which case the ordering BD = ^{D}UTU- + *išḫā-*, the customary form of address to the king by his subjects,[36] is obligatory:

A ← B (A:PN + B:KING, GOD, PROFESSION)
B ← D (B:KING, GOD, PROFESSION + D:GENERAL TERMS OF ADDRESS)

Hittite	AB	^{d}*Ḫalmašuiz*	***šiuš=miš***
		Ḫalmašuiz	**god=my**
			(CTH 1.46f.)
	BD	^{d}UTU-*e*	***išḫā=mi***[37]
		sun.god-VOC	**lord=my**
			(KUB 31.127 I 1)

The syntagm "^{D}UTU- + *išḫā-*" is significant in that it is abundantly attested (in this order) for all case forms (often even within the same text, e.g. texts no. 46 [Hagenbuchner 1989: 76f.] and no. 65, left margin 1-4 [Hagenbuchner 1989: 102f.]). A wealth of examples can be extracted from Hagenbuchner (1989).

In Tocharian, *ñakte/ñkät* 'god' is rigidly postposed to proper names, yielding the type AB; but if 'god' occurs with a C-item like '(wo)man' or a D-item like the general title *käṣṣi* 'master' it is moved to the left, i.e.

34 = DINGIR.MEŠ LÚ.MEŠ.

35 Under the premise that *šiuneš* (DINGIR.MEŠ) is a noun in apposition and not a purely graphic determinative.

36 Cf. Hagenbuchner (1989:150) and passim on the greeting formula in letters. For more such examples, see Güterbock (1956 [10.4]: 122-124).

37 = ^{D}UTU^{ŠI} BĒLI-YA.

A ← B (A:PN + B:KING, GOD, PROFESSION)
B ← C (B:KING, GOD, PROFESSION + C:KINSHIP TERM, GENDER/AGE)
B ← D (B:SOCIAL STATUS, PROFESSION + D:GENERAL TERMS OF ADDRESS)
A ←B ← C (A:PN +B:KING, GOD, PROFESSION + C:KINSHIP TERM, GENDER/AGE)

Tocharian A	AB	*humā-ṃ*	***ñäkteṃñā-ṃ***
		Huma-OBL	**goddess-OBL**
			(A201a2)
Tocharian B	BC	*ñäkteñña-na*	***klai-na-nts***
		goddesses-OBL.PL.F	**woman-OBL.PL.F-GEN**
			(BH149add.122a4)
Tocharian B	BC	*kapyār-i*	***śrāy*** ***klaiy-na***
		worker-NOM.PL	**adult.man:NOM.PL** **woman-NOM.PL.F**
			(SI B Toch./9, 11)[38]
Tocharian A	BD	*yaṃtrācāre-ṃ*	***käṣṣi-n-ā***
		artisan-OBL	**master-OBL-PERL**[39]
			(A 8a1)
Tocharian B	BD	*pañäkte*	***käṣṣi***
		Buddha:NOM	**master:NOM**
			(BH149.038b1)
Tocharian B	BD	*poyśi*	***käṣṣi***
		all.knowing.one:NOM	**master:NOM**
		(No 34, 43, 361.1 [Schmidt 1998:75], 54 [Schmidt 1998:78])	
Tocharian B	BD	*poyśi*	***saswe***
		all.knowing.one:NOM	**sir:NOM**
			(B108b2)

[38] Exceptions to the postposing of 'man/woman' generics in Tocharian do occur, e.g., West Tocharian *āl yriye* 'male (being), lamb', *klaina śroñ* 'females, kids' (Pinault 1998: 12). These pairings do not seem do comply with the hyponym-hyperonym order postulated for SOV languages; rather, they show the converse order, i.e., *āl yriye* 'male (being), lamb' = **generic**-specific = [**male being** [lamb]]. Nonetheless, the examples cited can be understood as being in accordance with the expected hyponym-hyperonym order if the principal focus is shifted from the species to the gender, in which case the syntagm could be parsed as [[male] **lamb (indifferent to gender)**] = specific-**generic**.

[39] = perlative.

This leftward hyponymic relocation can be shown to apply iteratively. Owing to the fact that hyponymity and hyperonymity are not absolute but relative concepts, the same noun may function simultaneously both as a subordinate and as a superordinate. Thus within a noun-noun apposition of the left-branching AB-type, e.g. proper name + 'god', the B-item, 'god', is superordinate; but it is subordinate when juxtaposed to a C- or D-type item, like 'brother' or 'master', and consequently appears on the left. In Tocharian, the term 'prince' is required to follow the personal name but to precede the generic kinship term 'brother':

Tocharian A	AB	*nande*	***mäśkit***	
		Nanda:NOM.SG	**prince**:NOM.SG	
				(A108b2+)
	AB	*nande*	***mäśkit-e***	
		Nanda:GEN.SG	**prince**:GEN.SG	
				(A143b4+)
	ABC	*śākki-ñ*	***mäśkit-āñ***	*pracr-e*
		Śakyas-NOM.PL	**prince**-NOM.PL	brothers-NOM.PL
				(A 117b1)

Likewise, the term 'god' is required to follow the personal name but to precede the honorific term of address 'master':

Tocharian A	AB	*Metrakäṃ*	*ptā**ñkät***	
		Maitreya	**buddha.god**	
				(A 256 a6)
	ABD	*Metrak*	*ptā**ñkät***	*käṣṣi*
		Maitreya	**buddha.god**	master
				(A 305b1&5; MSN II.5b3f.)

A glance outside the Indo-European language family reveals that the correlation between semantic dependency relations and appositional word order applies to non-Indo-European languages too. In Hungarian, it is normal for the designation of a profession to follow the name of an individual (A+B), e.g *Sándorfi **tanár***, literally *Sándorfi **teacher***. However, if this same term 'teacher' occurs with the more general term *úr* 'mister', it is moved one place to the left: thus *Sándorfi **tanár*** becomes *Sándorfi **tanár** úr* (A+B+D), literally 'Sándorfi teacher mister'.

Hungarian	AB	*Sándorfi*	***tanár***	
		Sándorfi	**teacher**	
	ABD	*Sándorfi*	***tanár***	*úr*
		Sándorfi	**teacher**	mister

(Bárczi 2001: 489)

In much the same fashion, in Basque, the designation of a profession must follow a proper name, but again it is relocated to the left by a more general title such as 'mister/lord'.[40]

Basque	AB	*Zeus*	***jainko**-a*	
		Zeus	**god**-DET	
	BD	***jainko***	*jaur-a*	
		God	**lord.mister**-DET	

(cf. King & Elordi 1996: 53)

Basque	AB	*Müller*	***irakasle**-a*	
		Müller	**teacher**-DET	
	ABD	*Müller*	***irakasle***	*jaur-a*
		Müller	**teacher**	lord.mister-DET

In cases like the preceding, where appositional syntagms are composed of more than two nouns, the ordering of relative hyponyms and hyperonyms is continuous, i.e., it requires a given hyponym to be adjacent to its relative hyperonym; the resulting sequence must not be interrupted. For instance, in the above cases sequences like A+B+C, A+B+D are permitted, whereas sequences like A+C+B or A+D+B may not occur. What this all amounts to is that there is a kind of semantic chaining at work, requiring the adjacency (juxtaposition) of relative hyponyms to their relative hyperonyms. In this way, linear order is determined by hierarchical adjacency principles of semantic dependency.

---

40 More examples can of course be found, e.g. from Korean and Japanese. Ronald Kim (p.c.) draws my attention to Korean:

AB	*Kim=seonsaeng*	'Kim-teacher'
ABD	*Kim=seonsaeng=nim*	'Kim-teacher-Mr(s)'.

7. Close apposition and nominal classifiers outside Indo-European

In what follows, I will examine how the above results can be applied to languages that have grammaticalized a noun classifier system. The first question is whether the postposing of generic appositions described for OV languages, and the preposing in VO languages, is mirrored in the positional characteristics of noun classifiers. The second question is whether the phenomenon of adjacency of relative hyponyms and hyperonyms might recur among languages with grammaticalized noun classifiers.

7.1. Nominal classifiers and word order

We first examine whether there might be an association between head-final syntax and postposed classifiers, and head-initial syntax and preposed classifiers. We begin by briefly surveying a few languages. The following results, of course, can only be provisional and are intended to show that further research in this area might be promising. There are languages which show the expected correlation of head-initial word-order profile and preposed classifiers. Among these are the Mayan languages Jacaltec and Acatec, both of which have VSO word order and prepose their classifiers.[41] Likewise, the Austronesian language Kilivila, which is VOS, has preposed classifiers, cf. Senft (1996: 20, 22, 353), Heine & Kuteva (2002: 207).

There are, however, cases with mixed word-order patterns which are more difficult to assess. A case in point is furnished in southern Africa by non-Khoe Khoisan languages where, in the NP, most modifiers follow the head noun, but associative (and appositional) constructions show the reverse, head-final order. For example, the southern Khoisan language !Xoô expresses natural gender through the postposed nouns 'father', 'mother':

!Xoô	*gùmi*	*à̰a*
	cattle	**father** (= ox)
	gùmi	*qáe*
	cattle	**mother** (= cow) mother

(Güldemann 1999: 69, Heine & Kuteva 2002: 133)

---

[41] Cf. Craig (1986: 264) on Jacaltec: "Noun classifiers (N Cl) are free morphemes which immediately precede the noun and may co occur with the various other determiners of the noun phrase, such as numeral, possessive, and demonstrative". For Acatec, see Zavala (2000: 117ff.), and cf. also Heine & Kuteva (2002: 208, 313f.).

If analyzed as an appositive syntagm, this type of NP accords well with the cases of postposed kinship terms cited above (p. 12f.) for Indo-European and non-Indo-European SOV-type languages. However, these examples also allow an analysis as a juxtapositional genitive construction, as Tom Güldemann informs me: that is, 'cattle-mother', to be understood as 'the mother of cattle', which then develops into 'female cattle'. Of course, if we are truly dealing with a possessive NP, the parallel with the appositional syntagms would be invalidated. Nevertheless, the question arises whether an alternative synchronic analysis as a non-possessive, purely appositional NP might also be possible, i.e., 'cattle mother', to be understood not as 'mother of cattle' but as 'cattle which are or can be mothers'. A parallel to such a sex-marking and non-possessive use of 'mother' can be found in compounds like English *mother-bird* or German *Mutter-tier*, 'animal which is a mother', and *Mutter-schaf*, 'sheep which is a mother'.

The generic-specific construction found in many Australian languages would seem to be another ideal test case for our purposes. Nevertheless, it is once again difficult to assess this type. Many Australian languages, including Yidiny, have no strictly defined word-order profile. The statistically preferred word order of Yidiny is OV, but obliques tend to follow the verb, and in principle, all word orders are possible (Dixon 1977: 268f.), cf. e.g.

Yidiny	*bama:l*	*yaburuŋgu*	*minya*	*gangu:l*	***wawa:l***
	person.CLF	girl	animal.CLF	wallaby	**see:PAST**

"The (person) girl saw the (animal) wallaby."

Yidiny	*minya*	*gangu:l*	***jana-ng***	*jugi-il*	*gabuma-la*
	animal.CLF	wallaby	**stand-PRS**	tree.CLF -LOC	black_pine-LOC

"The (animal) wallaby is standing by the (tree) black pine."

(Dixon 1977: 480, Wilkins 2000: 166)

As for the generic–specific construction, Dixon observes (2002: 457) that "[a] generic noun will most frequently precede a specific noun in an NP". This contradicts our expectation that OV word order ought to imply postposed generic nouns. However, Dixon adds that "most Australian languages have fair freedom of word order so that the alternative sequence is likely to be possible." Along these lines, there are also Australian languages that attest to a specific-generic order (alongside generic-specific constructions). Two such cases are Nyangumarta and Kayardild (cf. Dixon 2002: 457 with references).

7.2. Adjacency of relative hyponym and relative hyperonym

The second question is whether the phenomenon of the obligatory adjacency of a relative hyponym and its relative hyperonym can also be observed among languages with incipient (e.g. Arrernte) or grammaticalized (e.g. Yidiny) noun classification systems. Once again, Australian languages provide test cases. Here it "is possible to find two generic nouns co-occurring with a specific noun in an NP" (Dixon 1977: 247). The relevant cases can be subdivided into two types.

A) The specific noun is preceded by two inherent nature classifiers, such as PERSON + MAN, allowing a semantic analysis as a true hyperonym-hyponym relationship, since every man is a person.

(a) Yidiny	*bama*	***wagu:ɖa***	***wuɽgun***
	PERSON	MAN	**pubescent_boy**
	GENERIC HYPERONYM	GENERIC HYPONYM	SPECIFIC HYPONYM
			(Dixon 1977: 484)
(b) Yidiny	*bama*	***buɲa***	***yabu:ɽ***
	PERSON	WOMAN	**pubescent_girl**
	GENERIC HYPERONYM	GENERIC HYPONYM	SPECIFIC HYPONYM
			(Dixon 1977: 248)

B) In the second type, the specific noun is preceded by a function/use classifier (e.g., ARTEFACT) and an inherent nature classifier, such as STONE.[42] Here, in contrast to the first type, the relation of the two classifiers is not a true hyperonym-hyponym relationship but a sequence of pseudo-hyperonym plus hyponym, since the inherent nature property need not automatically imply the property of the function/use assignment (for instance, not every stone is an artefact).

(c) Arrernte	*arne*	***pwerte***	***athere***
	ARTEFACT	STONE	**grinding_stone**
	FUNCTION/USE	GENERIC HYPONYM	SPECIFIC HYPONYM

---

42 "Cooccurrence of classifiers is governed by the following principle. If two classifiers cooccur, one of them must be an inherent nature classifier, and the other has to refer to 'function/use'" (Dixon 1977: 484, Aikhenvald 2000: 83).

(d) Arrernte	*kere*	***thipe***	***njiŋke***
	EDIBLE MEAT	**BIRD**	**zebra_finch**
	FUNCTION/USE	GENERIC HYPONYM	SPECIFIC HYPONYM

(Wilkins 1989: 108, Dixon 2002: 457)

Now both the Yidiny and Arrernte examples can be analyzed as containing a rightward relocation of hyponyms. In example (b), the linear order of the three items can be parsed as hyperonym 'person' plus hyponym 'woman', which in turn functions as a hyperonym of the more specific final item 'pubescent girl'. Turning to Arrernte, example (d), we begin with the generic entity of 'edible meat', then select 'bird meat',[43] and finally narrow down 'bird meat' to 'meat of the zebra finch'. In example (c), we begin with the entire class of artefacts, then select those instruments made of stone, and finally narrow this choice down to 'grinding stone'.

Under this analysis, we obtain a model of rightward relocation of hyponyms which is the mirror image of the left relocation described above for languages such as Hungarian and Basque. Despite the difference in direction of branching, the two relocation patterns have one common denominator. They both follow the adjacency principle outlined above: hyponyms are juxtaposed to their relative hyperonyms. Thus, example (b) displays an order with continuously ascending specificity, while a discontinuous order of the type *PERSON + **pubescent girl** + WOMAN = GENERIC HYPERONYM + **specific** + GENERIC HYPONYM is excluded. As for (c) and (d), Wilkins (1989: 108) observes "a strict ordering of function/use classifier before inherent nature classifier". In other words, a discontinuous order of the type HYPERONYM + **FUNCTION-USE** + HYPONYM, e.g., BIRD + **EDIBLE MEAT** + ZEBRA FINCH or STONE + **ARTEFACT** + GRINDING STONE, is prohibited. Put differently, there appears to be a crosslinguistic rule which requires the hyperonym (*bird/stone*) to be adjacent to its relative hyponym (*zebra finch/grinding stone*).

In both the Yidiny and Arrernte cases, the obligatory adjacency of generic and specific classifiers corresponds to that of relative hyponym and hyperonyms in constructions with double apposition (cf. p. 40).

43 Cf. Wilkins's (2000: 199) glossing of *thipe* as 'flying fleshy food'.

8. Close apposition as a source of classifiers

As noted above (§ 1 ad fin.), with the exception of certain modern Indo-Aryan languages, the Indo-European family has never developed a grammatical system of noun classifiers. Nevertheless, closer inspection reveals the existence of noun-noun syntagms that can be regarded as the germ of a developmental continuum potentially leading to fully grammaticalized noun classifiers.

8.1. A pragmatic account of appositional generics

A number of languages can be adduced that conventionalize close appositions in the sociocultural sphere. For instance, Homeric Greek[44] and Biblical Hebrew show a certain predilection for PROPER NOUN – COMMON NOUN collocations involving the generic terms for 'man/woman'. The existence of such collocations is especially significant in light of the fact that lexemes signifying 'man/woman' are typologically frequent sources of classifiers and morphemes denoting natural and grammatical gender, cf. Aikhenvald (2000: 358) and §2.1.D above with fn. 9.

Left-branching NP	**Right-branching NP**
Homeric Greek	Biblical Hebrew[45]
φύλακάς τ' **ἄνδρας**, δμωάς τε **γυναῖκας**	**'īš** *kohēn*
'guardians **men** and servants **women**'	'**man** priest'
(Il. 9.477)	(Lev. 21.9)
τέκτονες **ἄνδρες**	**'īš** *sārīs*
'carpenters **men**'	'**man** eunuch'
(Il. 6.315 13.390)	(Jer. 38.7)
θηρήτορας **ἄνδρας**	**'īš** *śar wə-šōp̄ēṭ*
'hunters **men**'	'**man** prince and judge'
(Il. 9.544)	(Ex. 2.14)
Cf. above p. 14f. (§2.1D), p. 36f. (§6) on Hittite, p. 38 (§6) on Tocharian, and below p. 53ff. (§9.2).	Cf. above §2.2.1 on Old Church Slavonic.

44 Cf. already La Roche (1893: 201-203). A Homeric inventory has been given in section §2.1.D above.

45 For further instances, see Gesenius 33 (= BDB 35) on *'īš* and Gesenius 70 (= BDB 61) on *'iššāh*.

While the generics ('man/woman') in the above cases retain their status as free word forms, there are other cases in which apposed generics are cliticized. And in at least one such case, that of the Tocharian generic term for 'god', we can observe such a cliticized generic spread to an entire sociocultural class (theonyms), thus turning into a bound morpheme, which however has not yet crossed the boundary to become a grammatical morpheme.

As for the cliticization of postposed appositions, one may further compare the isolated case of German *Hérr Gótt*, which had already undergone univerbation in Early Modern German to yield a new composite noun ***Hérr**-gott* (i.e., MHG *herre gót* > Early Modern German *herrgot* > Modern German *Hérrgott*), cf. *Hérrgotts-frühe* (lit. 'Lord-God early', i.e. 'at the crack of dawn'). In other cases, such cliticized close appositions show what looks like an incipient spread to some but not all items of the same lexical field. A paradigmatic example is the partial spread of the apposed title *pater* in Latin theonyms. Starting from Latin *Diēs pater*, the lexical renewal of the inherited theonym *Iūpiter*, we observe the spread of *pater* and enclitic *-piter* to additional theonyms, so as to generate *Saturnus-pater, Ianus-pater, Mars-pater* > *Marspiter* (cf. Gellius 5.12.4f.). Finally, Tocharian B has gone one step further, generalizing the apposed common noun *ñákte* 'god' in its cliticized form *-ñäkte* to all theonyms, e.g. *kaún ñákte* > ***kaún**-ñäkte* 'sun-god'; for an inventory of forms see Winter (1987), Hackstein (2006: 104).

8.2. Function

In order to determine the position of the aforementioned collocations on a scale extending from purely lexical to fully grammatical, the textual and pragmatic context must be taken into consideration. Previous research has determined a number of possible functions of classifiers, cf. in general Aikhenvald (2000: 317-330):

a) highlighting: Rather than adding additional information, classifiers may serve as pure highlighting devices, tagging thematically important participants in foregrounded discourse; cf. Zavala (2000: 143) on Acatec.

b) referencing, anaphora: Classifiers may serve as markers of referentiality, resembling third-person pronouns in Indo-European languages; cf. Grinevald (2002: 266) on Jacaltec.

c) individuation: Classifiers are used when reference to a particular individual is required (Aikhenvald 2000: 318).

8.2.1. Homeric Greek

In fact, although the Homeric Greek appositional use of ἀνήρ 'man' is far from being grammaticalized, it exhibits some interesting functional overlap with the discourse-pragmatic functions of noun classifiers. In a number of languages, noun classifiers may indicate topicality, cf. Aikhenvald (2000: 322f.). Topicality, in turn, can be shown to be a property of Homeric NPs with apposed ἀνήρ:

a) The generic ἀνήρ can be apposed to new referents that are being introduced and that will be important in the text. In Il. 17.466, thematic emphasis is placed on a new referent: "But at last there was one of his companions (= ἑταῖρος **ἀνήρ**) who laid eyes upon him: Alkimedon, the son of Laerkes, descended from Haimon" (Lattimore). In Od. 6.3, at the beginning of the section dealing with Odysseus's arrival in Phaeacia, the first mention is made of the Phaeacians, Φαιήκων **ἄνδρων**, who play a central role in the sixth book. Later, in Od. 6.34f, on second mention, the common noun ἄνδρων is omitted.

b) The generic noun ἀνήρ can be apposed to pragmatically salient NPs. In a significant number of cases, specific-generic pairings involving ἀνήρ form part of similes, marking the standard of comparison, e.g., Il. 23.845 ὅσσον τις... βουκόλος **ἀνήρ** 'as far as an oxherd [**man**]', Od. 10.278 νεηνίῃ **ἀνδρὶ** ἐοικώς 'resembling a youth [**man**]'.

c) Aside from marking topicality, the apposing of ἀνήρ can serve to express individuation, e.g., Il. 9.544 πολλέων ἐκ πολίων θηρήτορας **ἄνδρας** ἀγείρας 'assembling together many hunting **men** out of numerous cities'.

8.2.2. Biblical Hebrew

Turning now to Biblical Hebrew, it is interesting to note that the generics *ʾīš* 'man', *ʾiššāh* 'woman', and *naʿărāh* 'girl' are sometimes apposed to new referents that are being introduced, e.g. at the beginning of a subsection: Jer 38.7 *wayyišmaʿ ʿeḇeḏ-meleḵ hakūšī* ***ʾīš sārīs*** *wəhū bəḇèṯ hammeleḵ* ... 'Now when Ebedmelech the Ethiopian, **a eunuch (man)** who was in the king's house, heard ...'; 1 Kg 17.10 *wəhinnēh-šām* ***ʾiššāh ʾalmānāh*** *məqošešeṯ ʿēṣīm* 'behold, **a widow (woman)** was there gathering sticks'; Jdg 4.4 *ūḏəḇōrāh* ***ʾiššāh nəḇīʾāh*** *ʾēšeṯ lapīḏōṯ hī šōp̄əṭāh ʾeṯ-yiśrāʾēl bāʿēṯ hahī* 'and Deborah, **a prophetess (woman)**, the wife of Lapidoth, she judged Israel at that time'; Jdg 21.12 *wayyimṣəʾū miyyōšəḇè yāḇèš gilèʿāḏ ʾarbaʿ mēʾōṯ* ***naʿărāh ḇəṯūlāh*** *ʾăšer loʾ- yāḏʿāh ʾīš ləmiškaḇ zāḵār* 'and they found among the inhabitants of Jabeshgilead four hundred young **virgins (girls)**, that had known no man by lying with any male'.

Neither in Homeric Greek nor in Biblical Hebrew has the discourse-pragmatic use of generics signifying 'man/woman/girl' become grammaticalized. Rather, it seems more appropriate to speak of an occasional tendency for certain generics to be collocated with specific nouns under certain discourse-pragmatic conditions. Unlike noun classifiers, such collocations are not obligatory, nor do the generics in such pairings recur in (anaphoric) referencing function. On the other hand, such occasional discourse devices do concretely attest the precursor constructions that have been hypothesized by typologists for the emergence of noun classifiers.

Returning to our initial question whether additional criteria can be brought forward in support of the presumed relationship between close apposition and noun classifiers, we may now conclude that such criteria do exist. First, the phenomenon of semantic subordination recurs both with close appositions and with grammaticalized classifiers. Second, certain positional (syntactic) characteristics such as the pre- and postposing dichotomy may be shared by close appositions and noun classifiers. Both of these observations merit further investigation.

9. Nominal apposition in ancient Indo-European. From casual to habitual collocation, from habitual collocation to grammatical construction

Although ancient Indo-European never developed a grammaticalized system of nominal classifiers, it can nevertheless be shown to have sporadically begun to functionalize noun-noun collocations. These can be arranged along a gradient ranging a) from casual to habitual collocation, and b) from habitual collocation to grammatical construction. Especially instructive are cases in which the transition between these two pairs can be demonstrated for the same phrase, thus illustrating the consecutive processes of phraseologization and syntacticization.

Casual collocation	Habitual collocation	Syntactic construction
phraseologization		syntacticization

- grammaticalization +

Prior to embarking on the study of specific cases, it will be useful to briefly set out the distinguishing features of the three stages, for these criteria will prove useful further below.

The development sketched above begins with the collocation of two nouns. At this stage, neither noun shows a particular predilection for being associated with the other or necessitates the presence of the other.

As the two nouns develop a tendency to be combined, their collocation develops from an occasional into a habitual one. At the same time, the process of habitualization is marked by a decrease in paradigmatic variability. At this stage, the occurrence of the habitual collocation is dependent solely on semantic (and not yet dictated by morphosyntactic) factors.

This changes when syntacticization takes place. With the change of the habitual collocation to a syntactic construction, morphosyntactic rules require the appositional noun to be employed. To take an example, in languages with grammaticalized numeral classifiers, the counting of non-human objects requires the numeral to cooccur with the non-human classifier (= the former appositional noun).

While no single ancient Indo-European language attests all three stages in the pathway just sketched, it is nevertheless possible to combine evidence from several Indo-European languages that attest the same semantically and even etymologically identical noun-noun appositional phrase at different developmental stages. Viewed together, these stages illustrate the entire process of both phraseologization and syntactization for the same model phrase. They show the potential for apposed generic nouns to become functionalized as grammatical elements and eventually provide the source for grammatical elements such as classifiers or even bound morphemes.

In the following, I shall present two such case studies dealing with NPs of the structure "numeral plus nominal apposition plus referent". The value of these two studies lies in the fact that they allow a glimpse of the situation prior to the grammaticalization of classifiers, and demonstrate noun-noun appositional syntagms to be a possible source in Indo-European for the grammaticalization of nominal classifiers.

9.1. Apposition in counting: numeral-apposition NPs

In fact, numeral-noun appositional syntagms are a frequently utilized syntactic template in counting. A typical format is the concatenation of a cardinal, an appositional noun and the nominal item counted, i.e., NUMERAL + APPOSITION + COUNTNOUN, where the apposition slot is filled by a noun denoting accessory or natural qualities of the counted noun. Given its semantics, this slot favors the conversion of the appositional noun to an adjective. As we shall see further below (§9.2.2.1.2.), this change in syntactic constituency has further repercussions for the placement of the appositional noun.

9.1.1. YOKE >> PAIR

An instructive example is furnished by the IE lexeme **i̯eu̯g(-es)-, i̯ug-om* 'yoke'. This noun originally signified a pair of yoked draught animals, cf. Old Lat. *iuga boverum* 'pairs of oxen' (Cato *Agr.* 62.1), *boum iuga duo* (Varro *R.* 1.19.1), Homeric Greek ζεύγεα 'yokes of draught animals plowing a field' (*Il.* 18.543), but then was extended to designate pairs of any animate referent and eventually to any pair.

Widespread among ancient Indo-European languages is the use of numeral plus the noun 'yoke' in apposition plus counted referent.[46] As we shall see below, this syntactic construction is indeed the precursor of numeral-classifier constructions as found in certain modern Indo-Aryan languages. In ancient Indo-European, this collocational type is still patently phraseological. The phraseological status of the numeral-plus-'yoke' construction is very likely an archaism of PIE date in light of its cross-linguistic attestation and word-formational behavior; alongside the noun-noun appositional type, e.g. "two yokes/pairs [of] oxen", there exists the nominalized version, a substantival compound made up of numeral plus 'yoke'. This compositional type is the word-formational version of the free collocational type, and as such presupposes the existence of the noun-noun appositional type. I will proceed with documentation of the relevant data.

---

46 These collocations display the word 'yoke' in either of three stem forms: beside **i̯ugóm*, there occurs the root noun **i̯eu̯g-/*i̯ug-* and an s-stem **i̯eu̯g-es-* (Gr. ζεῦγος, Lat. *iugera*). Regarding the cooccurrence of root noun and *s*-stem, cf. PIE **u̯et-*, **u̯et-e/os-* 'year', **u̯ek^{w}-*, **u̯ek^{w}-e/os-* 'voice') and Schindler (1979: 58f.) "*s*-Stämme neben WN sind häufig".

Examples of the appositional employment of 'yoke' in the sense of 'pair' come from Old Hittite, Mycenean and Old Latin:

1 YOKE: NP. Hittite: LÚ^{MEŠ} ^{URU}*Lum-na-ḫi-la* **1 *i-ú-kán*** *ú-iz[-zi]* "men from Lumnahila, one pair, is coming" (KBo 12.131 r. Kol. 5', Rieken 1999: 62).

Mycenean: *Aiwolos Kelainos k^{w}e ne(woi), we(rgatai) BOS^{m}* ***ZE(ugos)*** **1** = *g^{w}oṷe(s) d^{z}eṷgos hem* "Aiwolos and Kelainos, young oxen, draught animals, one yoke" (KN Ch 896, Hiller 1986: 257, Bartoněk 2003: 507).

3 YOKES: NP. Hittite: $^{LÚ.MEŠ}$ḪÚB.BI **III *i-ú-uk*** *ú-en-zi* "dancers, three pairs are coming" (KBo 25.72 r. Kol. 11'f., see Rieken 1999: 61f. and Groddek 2004: 18 [text], 19 [transl.], 35 [comm.] ad Vs. II 20) with root noun *i-ú-uk* in the (generic) distributive singular. For this construction in Hittite, see Hoffner (2007: 332), Hoffner & Melchert (2008: 158f.).

5, 6 YOKES: NP >> AdjP. There is one instance of a numeral-plus-'yoke' NP being converted into an adjective phrase (AdjP) classifying a further noun: Old Latin *sī* ***sex iugīs*** *vāsīs opus est* "in case there is need for six pairwise connected (olive-pressing) plants" (Cato *Agr.* 145.1).[47] This instance is of particular interest because it provides the exact match on the phraseological level of what was later to emerge on the syntactic level as the numeral-plus-classifier construction in modern Indo-Aryan languages. As such, it illustrates the gradient leading from collocational phraseology to syntactic construction.[48]

9.1.1.1. Cooccurrence of noun phrase and dvigu compound

We frequently find the cooccurrence of noun phrases of the type NUMERAL+NOUN and the compounded version thereof, signifying ‚having X items' or 'aggregate of X items', the so-called *dvigu* compounds. The two types are closely linked derivationally, so that the presence of a *dvigu* compound indicates the (prior) existence of the corresponding numeral-plus-noun phrase, cf. e.g.

---

47 Cf. in an enumeration *vāsa oleāria īnstrūcta* ***iuga quīnque*** "olive-pressing plants, equipped, pairwise five" (Cato *Agr.* 10.2).

48 In the same vein, Lehmann 2000 draws attention to Modern German collocations like *drei Mann Besatzung* 'three-man crew' (cf. §. 1 above on Jalcatec *naj Pel* = man.CLF Peter 'Peter'), *drei Stück Vieh* 'three head of cattle.' Typologically, collocations like these furnish the semantic and syntactic prototypes for grammaticalized numeral-noun classifier constructions for animate items, as attested for a wealth of non-Indo-European languages.

NOUN-PHRASE VERSION NUMERAL + NOUN NP 'X YOKES'	COMPOUND VERSION NUMERAL-NOUN COMPOUND 'AGGREGATE OF X YOKES'
*du̯(o)i̯h$_1$ i̯ugoi̯h$_1$ 'two yokes'	*du̯i-i̯ugom *du̯oi̯o-i̯ugom
*trih$_2$ i̯ugeh$_2$ 'three yokes'	*tri-i̯ugom
*k^{w}etu̯ōr i̯ugeh$_2$ 'four yokes'	*k^{w}etu̯r̥-i̯ugom

2-YOKE: CP. Homeric Greek δίζυγες ἵπποι (Il. 5.195, 10.473);
Latin *bīgae* 'team of two chariot-horses' (Varro *L.* 8.55, 10.24, *ThLL* 2.1981-3);
Cf. Hittite: *tāyuga-/dāyuga-* 'two years old' (**du̯oi̯o-i̯ugom*), see Eichner (1992: 56f.), Rieken (1999: 150 fn. 704.).

3-YOKE: CP. Latin *trīgae* (Varro *L.* 8.55) 'team of three chariot-horses';
Cf. Vedic *tri-yugám* 'span of three ages' (RV 10.97,1).

4-YOKE: CP. Old Latin *quadrīgae*: *quadrigas* (Varro *L.* 8.55, 10.24, Cic. *Or.* 157);
Cf. Vedic *catur-yúj-* 'yoked by four' (RV 8.6,48), *cátur-yuga-* '[chariot] having four yokes' (RV 2.18,1).

The inflection of the nouns *bīgae, trīgae, quadrīgae* may conceal an archaism. The nouns *bīgae, trīgae, quadrīgae*, while assigned to the feminine plural in Old Latin, are replaced by the overtly marked singular forms *bīga, trīga, quadrīga* in the post-Augustean period, see Kühner & Holzweissig (1912: 504). This indicates that, despite their plural inflection, the forms *bīgae, trīgae, quadrīgae* were conceived of as singular forms (like Lat. *tenebrae* = fem. pl. Vedic *támisrāḥ*). Given this perception of *bīgae*, etc. as singular forms, the likeliest explanation for Latin singular collectives in *–ae* (otherwise preserved in Latin only in the pronominal declension as feminine singular or as neuter plural, cf. *haec, quae*) is to identify them with archaic singular collectives of the type PIE **-eh$_2$-i* or PIE **-eh$_2$-i-t* > **-eh$_2$-i-d*, a complex collective suffix composed of collective **–eh$_2$-* plus abstract-collective **–i* and optionally further enlarged by the collective suffix **-t* as encountered in **déḱm̥-t* (cf. Rau 2009:48). The idea that Latin neuter plural *–ae* conceals a collective suffix is implicit already in Johannes Schmidt's equation of Latin nom. acc. n. pl. QUAI (CIL 1^2.583.34), Osc. **pai, paí** with Pruss. *kai* 'what' (Schmidt 1889: 227f.). The suffix in question was later shown by Eichner (1973: 59f.) and Watkins (1971: 55 fn. 5, 1975: 364f.) to be productive in Anatolian (Luvian *ḫattula**ḫ**it* 'health', *ašrula**ḫ**it* 'femininity', cf. Starke 1990: 153-76, Rieken 1999: 262, Rau 2009: 49 fn. 35) and Homeric Greek (βασιλη̈ΐς with –ς from *-*ts*, i.e., collective *-*t* plus individualizing *-*s*, reanalysed as *-*ds*; cf. gen. βασιληΐδος with secondary -δ-, as in the collective noun Greek δεκάς, -άδος, Skt. *daśat-* from PIE **déḱm̥-t-s*). To conclude, the Latin nouns *bīgae, trīgae, quadrīgae* descend from transnumeral collectives whose assignment to singular or plural was language-specific, as is the case with other collectives, cf. Hitt. *widār* (pl.) vis-à-vis Greek ὕδωρ (sg.) and Nussbaum (1986: 127).

9.2. Apposition as sex-marking strategy, and numeral classifiers

The same picture is obtained with collocations of the type "numeral plus appositional noun denoting 'man' or 'woman' plus counted objects". As we saw above, apposing the generic terms for 'man' and 'woman' is typologically among the most widespread techniques for sex marking outside Indo-European and a common source for human classifiers attached to numerals. It is noteworthy that a pre-grammaticalized, collocational version of this syntagm is widely present in ancient Indo-European languages. In the framework, these instances of numeral-plus-'man' collocations arouse even greater interest, for the entire range of the grammaticalization scale sketched above is attested across the individual ancient Indo-European languages.

Archaic Latin uses appositional *mās* 'male' and *fēmina* 'female' to mark sex with generic animal names. As for *mās* (*ThLL* 8.423f., s.v. *mās* III), note for instance ***ovī mārī*** *testiculī dēmptī sunt* (Varro *L.* 5.91), *Ianuī Quirinō* ***agnum mārem*** *caeditō* (Fest. p. 204 Lindsay), **bovem mārem** *Iovī optimō maximō proprium immolāvit* (CIL 6.32.323, 103), and *immolandum ... cui deō* ***māribus hostiīs****, cui* ***fēminīs*** (Cic. *leg.* 2.29); for appositional *fēmina*, see below §9.2.2.

9.2.1. MAN >> sex-marking morpheme

The developmental stages of collocations with numerals followed by 'man' are again attested, not within any single Indo-European language, but across the Indo-European family.

2 MEN: NP. Homeric Greek attests casual collocations, with no indication of further functionalization: δύο ἄνδρες 13.499, δύο δ' ἄνδρες Il. 18.498, δύο δ' ἀνέρες 20.158, δύο δ' ἄνδρε 20.286, ἄνδρε δύω 23.659=802.

By contrast, Latin employs collocations of the type *duovirī* (for a collection see Kühner & Holzweissig 1912: 502), which, despite their semantic resemblance to the Greek collocations, differ from the latter in showing all earmarks of habitualization. Evidence of their phraseological status is provided by a number of phonetic and morphological phenomena such as univerbation (*sex=virī* > *sēvirī*), the preservation of morphological archaisms, e.g., *duum=virum* (Cic. *Or.* 156) with archaic gen. pl. *duum* and *virum*; *trīs=virōs* with archaic acc. pl. *trīs* (for attestations, see below), and instances of backformation (gen. pl. *duum=virum* >> nom. sg. *duum=vir,* nom. pl. *sēvirī* >> *sēvir*).

3 MEN: NP. *trēs virī* 'board of three men, judges' (Pl. *Amph.* 155, Liv. 33.42.1); *trium virum* (Gell. 3.9.4, Cic. *Or.* 156, Cato apud Fest. p. 466 Lindsay, Varro apud Gell. 13.12.6); *trīs virōs* (Pl. *Pers.* 72, Cic. *de Orat.* 3.73).

6 MEN: NP. *sēvirī* 'members of an official board of six' (CIL 11.2647), *sēvir* (CIL 14.2795, Petron. 65.5).

7 MEN: NP. *septem=virum* (Gell. 1.12.6).

10 MEN: NP. *decem=virī, decem=virōs* (Cic. *R* 2.36).

15 MEN: NP. *quīndecim=virum* (Gell. 1.12.6, Tac. *Ann.* 6.12).

3 MEN: NP >> AdjP. As in the case of the numeral-plus-'yoke' collocation, there is evidence for the appositional use of the numeral-plus-'man' collocation as an adjective classifying a following head noun. A case in point is Liv. 33.42.1: *Rōmae eō prīmum annō* ***trēs virī*** *epulōnēs factī C. Licinius Lucullus ... , et P. Manlius et P. Porcius Laeca.* In this passage *trēs virī epulōnēs* occurs in the sense of 'three (men) banqueters'. The internal syntax of the passage is to be interpreted as "At Rome, appointed as the three banqueters (= the college of the three banqueters) were C. Licinius Lucullus ... , P. Manlius and P. Porcius Laeca."

In addition, the genitive plural ****trium virum*** *epulōnum* (cf. Gell. 1.12.6 ***septem virum*** *epulōnum*) serves as the basis for backforming a nominative singular ***trium=vir*** *epulō* (Liv. 40.42.7) and a dative singular *P. Cornēliō Dolabellae cos [cōnsul]* ***septem=virō*** *epulōnī* (CIL 3.1741). Instances like these show that the numeral-plus-*vir* collocation had ceased to be transparent as an appositional phrase consisting of numeral plus 'man' and was reanalyzed as an adjectival compound taking singular concord with *epulō.*

The foregoing observations help to clarify the syntactic interpretation of the following passage: *Sed ut pontificēs veterēs propter sacrificiōrum multitūdinem* ***trīs virōs epulōnēs*** *esse voluērunt, ...* "but as the old priests wished because of the multitude of sacrifices that there be three banqueters" (Cic. *de Orat.* 3.73). While there seems to be no way of rigorously excluding a copula construction (with either *trīs=virōs* or *epulōnēs* functioning as predicate of the other noun), the above examples tip the scales in favor of taking *trīs=virōs* + *epulōnēs* as an adjective phrase plus head noun, and *esse* as an existential verb 'there exist(s)'.

6 MEN: NP >> AdjP. Syntactic parallels to *trīs=virōs epulōnēs* and *septem=virō epulōnī* are furnished by *sēvirī Augustālēs* (CIL 14.367) 'six (men) priests of Augustus' and *sēvirō Augustālī* (Petron. 30.2).

3 MEN: CLF, 4 MEN:CLF. Bengali has gone a step farther in syntacticizing the numeral noun appositional type exemplified by Latin *sex iugīs vasīs*, *trēs virī epulōnēs* and *sēviri Augustālēs*. In Bengali, the collocation of numeral and generic term for man/person has ceased to be phraseological. Instead, a syntactic rule requires a numeral referring to a human object to be followed by the human classifier *-jon*, *tin-**jon** śromik*, *car-**jon** śromik* 'three, four labourers'. It is even possible to concretely exemplify the lexicon-syntax continuum with (occasional) correspondences such as Vedic *mắnuṣo jánaḥ* '(hu)man being/person' (RV 6.2.3c) >> Assamese *manuɦ-zɒn* [man-DEF.HUMAN.CLF] 'the man' (see § 1. above) or Latin *trēs virī epulōnēs*, *septem virī epulōnēs* 'three, seven men banqueters/sacrificial priests' and Bengali *tin-jon purohit*, *śat-jon purohit* lit. 'three, seven (person.CLF) priests'.

phraseologization >> syntacticization

Casual collocation	Habitual collocation	Syntactic numeral-classifier construction
Gk. δύο ἄνδρες	Lat. *duovirī*	Bengali *dui-jon* + X 'two-person.CLF + HUMAN'
Gk. τρεῖς ἄνδρες	Lat. *trēs virī*, OIr. *triar*	Bengali *tin-jon* + X 'three-person.CLF + HUMAN'
Gk. τέτταρες ἄνδρες	Lat. *quattuor virī*, OIr. *cethrar*	Bengali *car-jon* + X 'four-person.CLF + HUMAN'

Habitual collocation	Syntactic numeral-classifier construction
Lat. *trēs virī epulōnēs*	Bengali *tin-jon purohit*
Lat. *septem virī epulōnēs*	Bengali *śat-jon purohit*

- grammaticalization +

9.2.1.1. Cooccurrence of noun phrase and dvigu compound

The cooccurrence of the noun phrase and the compound version documented above for collocations of the type “numeral plus ‘yoke’” recurs with the collocational type “numeral plus ‘man’”.

NOUN-PHRASE VERSION NUMERAL + NOUN NP ‘X MEN’	COMPOUND VERSION NUMERAL-NOUN COMPOUND ‘COLLEGE/BOARD OF X MEN’
*treie̯s u̯ih$_1$ro-es ‘three men’	*tri-u̯ih$_1$rom
*k$^u̯$etu̯ores u̯ih$_1$ro-es ‘four men’	*k^{w}etu̯r̥-u̯ih$_1$rom

Old Irish makes wide use of the compound version, thus indirectly presupposing the Latin collocational type. The so-called personal numerals of Old Irish, *triar, cethrar, cóicer, se(i)sser, ochtar, nónbor, de(i)chenbor* ‘three, four, five, six, eight, nine, ten persons’, continue old numeral compounds with PIE **u̯ih$_1$ro-* ‘college/board of X men’.[49] Historically, they are neuter *dvigu* compounds in **-om*, as reflected in the nasalization of the following word triggered by OIr. *ilar* ‘many’ from **pelh$_1$u-u̯ih$_1$ro-m*, and as exemplified by Latin *triduum* (< **tri-diu̯om*) ‘period of three days’, cf. Thurneysen (1946: 243f.), Greene (1992: 517-519), and Stifter (2006: 231f.).

Old Irish is peculiar in grammaticalizing not the noun-noun appositional type of Latin *trēs virī* as a classifier construction, but rather its compound version, e.g., OIr. *triar* ‘group/board of three men, three-man-hood, threesome’ going back to PIE **tri-u̯ih$_1$rom*. These compound numbers underwent morphologization as numeral pronouns, construed with the dependent genitive of the referent counted. The numeral pronouns of Old Irish came to develop uses functionally (though not structurally) equivalent to those of numeral classifiers. The desemanticization of the lexical component with the former meaning ‘man’ is not yet completed in Old Irish, cf. e.g.

3-MAN:CP. In keeping with their etymological connection with *fer* ‘man’, it is reasonable to assume that the Old Irish personal numbers were

---

[49] There are phonological problems: *nón-bor* is not the regular development of **nou̯en u̯iron*, which would have led us to expect **noínber* instead, cf. *noí*^{n} ‘nine’, *noínden* ‘nine days’. But analogy after *nomad* ‘ninth’, as suggested by Greene (1992: 518), provides a possible explanation.

originally used solely to signify 'a group of persons,' specifically 'adult men':

> *lotar dó a triur churad*
> go.PRT3PL to.3SG.N their three.person.DAT warrior.GENPL
> lit. "they went there, their triumvirate of warriors", "they, the three warriors went there" (LU 9033)

But already by the Old Irish period, the usage of the personal numbers had been extended to refer to female and human referents in general:

> *tánaicc Calcus ocus a thriar ban*
> come.PRT3SG Calcus and his threesome woman.GENPL
> "Calcus and his three wives came" (St. Ercuil 1952, Stifter 2006: 232)

Compare the Modern Irish usage of the substantive numeral to refer to male referents regardless of age:

> *triar mac*
> three.man son.GEN.PL
> 'three sons' (Greene 1992: 531).

Functionally, Old Irish *triar churad* 'three-man-hood of warriors' corresponds to the type illustrated by Latin *tres viri epulones* 'three men banqueters' = 'the college of three banqueters' or to the fully grammaticalized classifier type of Bengali. The co-occurrence of free collocation and its compound version can be projected back into PIE, e.g., PIE **tre̯ies u̯ih₁ro-es gʷr̥(H)-dʰh₁o-es*, literally 'three men bards' alongside synonymous **tri-u̯ih₁rom gʷr̥(H)-dʰh₁o-om*, literally 'three-man-hood of bards'.

9.2.2. WOMAN >> sex-marking morpheme

In Proto-Indo-European, natural feminine gender could be marked lexically by apposing the generic term for woman. This state of affairs continued through the Old Latin period, to judge by examples such as the following (*ThLL* 6.462f., s.v. *femina* II):

lupum ***fēminam*** (ascribed to Ennius [Enn. *Ann.* 68 and 70 Vahl.[2]] by Quintilian *Inst.* 1.6.12); in the description of a sacrifice *porcum* ***fēminam*** and *porco* ***fēminā*** (Cato *Agr.* 1.134.1), *porcō* ***fēminā*** *piāculum faciundum* (Cicero *Leg.* 2.57); also *leōnēs* ***fēminas*** (Gellius 13.7.3), ***fēminīs*** *būbus* (Varro *R.* 2.1.17), *agnus mās īdem* ***fēminaque*** (Liv. 28.11.3), *mās et* ***fēmina*** *aquila* (Varro *L.* 8.7).

9.2.2.1 PIE *(h_1)esōr 'woman' and the feminine of the cardinals 'three' and 'four' in Proto-Indo-European

The existence of the lexical and appositional encoding of natural feminine gender sheds new light on an old claim. In 1934 Benveniste, following Meringer (1904: 171f.), drew attention to word-formational traces of the lexeme for 'woman' (*(h_1e)sō̆r-, *(h_1e)ser-, *(h_1)sr-) as a feminine gender suffix. Benveniste (1934: 105f.) reconstructed Ved. *tísras*, Av. *tišrō* as the feminine form of the cardinal number 'three' **t(r)i* (with dissimilatory *r*-loss[50]) plus *(h_1e)s(o)res*, to be glossed as 'tres feminae'. The etymology proposed by Benveniste accounts for the zero-grade morpheme *-sr-* found in Sanskrit *tisrás*, *cátasras*, OIr. *téoir*, *cethéoir*, MWelsh *teir*, *pedeir*.[51]

Benveniste's proposal gains plausibility in light of the morphonologically even more transparent employment of the same lexeme to denote feminine gender in Hittite, e.g., *haššuš* 'king', *haššuššara-* 'queen' (see already Ehelolf 1936: 185f.), and is generally accepted today (cf. e.g. Rieken 1999: 262, Ledo-Lemos 2000: 133-145).

While Indo-Europeanists have concerned themselves mainly with further ascertaining the details of the morphonological reconstruction (Janda 1999: 320f., Rieken 1999: 262, Kim 2005: 128), the discussion by Oettinger (1986) goes a step further and sets out the details of the syntactic reconstruction. According to him (1986: 126), the employment of PIE *(h_1)esor-* 'woman' in the formation of the feminine cardinals 'three' and 'four' may preserve the remnants of a pre-inflectional stage, with the numeral left uninflected and the encoding of natural gender conveyed by the apposed generic term for woman ("Vielleicht sind daher *k^wét ésores*, *tr(é)i̯ ésores* als Zusammenrückungen zu betrachten, die ... als syntaktische Fügungen 'vier bzw. drei Frauen' bezeichneten. Die Möglichkeit unflektierter Zahlwörter wäre für dieses frühe Stadium nicht auszuschließen.") While Oettinger chose to be modest in his claim ("vielleicht"), the proposed pathway of development involving the apposition of 'woman' is immediately evident in light of the above

---

50 A precedent for such dissimilatory *r*-loss in PIE **tri-* is furnished by Avestan *tištriia-* 'complex of three stars' from **tri-štr-i̯a-* < **tri-$h_2$str-i̯o-* (Janda 2008: 489).

51 Phonologically, the Celtic forms descend from **tisres* and **k^wetesres*, as was established by Cowgill (1957: 341-345); for more details, see Kim (2008). But while resolving the question of the origin of the feminine marker *-sr-, it poses new questions regarding the morphophonemics of the compound numerals, in particular how to account for the unexpected zero grade, a question to be addressed below.

discussion. It seems not to have been noticed that a construction of the type "cardinal numeral plus 'woman' plus counted object" corresponds exactly to the attested syntactic template comprising numeral plus generic term for 'man/woman' and counted object, the ancient Indo-European phraseological precursor of the typologically very frequent numeral-classifier construction.

9.2.2.1.1. Reduction in univerbation

The one obstacle on the formal side of the etymology which needs additional treatment is the unexpected zero-grade in the assumed erstwhile plural form of 'woman'. For the plural of 'woman', PIE *(h_1)ésores* ought to be expected (the plural of amphikinetic PIE *(h_1)ésōr*, cf. Rieken 1999: 262f., Kim 2008: 145). This problem has resisted explanation so far, but it can be solved once it is recognized that the likeliness of unexpected zero-grades is heightened by morphonological and semantic factors. The phenomenon typically occurs in univerbation, and in particular in univerbations that belong to the core vocabulary.

Prior to setting out the details of this explanation, it will be necessary to digress briefly on the connection between frequency, functionalization and allegro phenomena. Irregular loss of vowels and syllables has been recognized as a side effect of lexical high-frequency items at least since Meillet's celebrated article of 1912. It was Meillet's insight (1912: 138f.) that an increase in functional load and frequency is often associated with allegro phenomena. This connection can be instructively demonstrated with miminal pairs contrasting the same or homophonous words in differing degrees of grammaticalization. In such pairs, allegro treatment is confined to the grammaticalized member of the pair. Functional load furthers the irregular loss of phonemes, including vowels, ablaut grades, obstruents, or entire syllables. To demonstrate the cooccurrence of functional load and allegro phenomena, compare the following minimal pairs:

			Allegro form
VERB	*She has a cat.*	*~~She's [= has] a cat.~~*	impossible
AUXILIARY	*She has done it.*	→ *She's done it.*	possible

(cf. Diewald 1997: 13)

			Allegro form
VERB	*He's going to school.*	*~~He's gonna school.~~*	impossible
AUXILIARY	*He is going to do it.*	→ *He's gonna do it.*	possible

(cf. Hopper & Traugott 2003: 1)

German			**Allegro form**
VERB	*Er isst es wirklich.* "He really eats it."	*~~Er iss-es wirklich.~~*	impossible
COPULA	*Er ist es wirklich.* "He really is it."	→ *Er iss-es wirklich.*	possible

The correlation to be drawn between functional load and irregular phonological reduction is likely connected to semantics, for an increase in function and a decrease in lexical meaning diminish the importance of individual phonemes and derivational morphemes, thus allowing them to be reduced and eventually to disappear.

The same phenomenon recurs on a syntactic level with syntactic formulas. In the course of grammaticalization, formulaic collocations tend to be "eroded" by the irregular loss of constituents, e.g. the loss of an otherwise mandatory article in the idiomatized *in the light of* >> *in light of*. The motivation behind this erosion is the same as with allegro phenomena: the loss of lexical meaning makes certain constituents dispensable. Syntactic condensation and allegro reduction in univerbation are phenomena of the same kind.

Returning to our initial question, it is therefore not coincidental that instances of irregular zero-grade can be found in PIE exactly in the domain of function words (numerals, adverbs and prepositions) and univerbated collocations involving function words.

(a) Univerbation of prepositional phrases. Cf. Nussbaum (1986: 82ff., 272), Forssman (2000: 51f.), e.g.

PIE *_ĝ^{h}esri_ >> *_ĝ^{h}sri_

The PIE prepositional phrase *_me ĝ^{h}esri_ (loc.) 'in/to the hand' yields adverbial/prepositional *_meĝ^{h}sri_ 'near' (Gk. μέχρι(ς) 'up to, as far as', Arm. *merj* 'near') with irregular vowel syncope in the second syllable, cf. Nussbaum (1986: 82f., 132).

PIE *d^hu̯er >> d^hur

The PIE prepositional phrase **prŏ̄ d^hu̯er* (loc.) 'before the door' results in adverbial **prŏ̄ d^hur* or **prŏ̄ d^hures* (abl.) 'out of the door' > **prŏ̄ d^hurs* > *prādúḥ* 'visible' (Forssman 2000: 51f.), again with irregular vowel syncope in the second syllable.

PIE *u̯eti >> *uti

The same applies to PIE **per u̯eti* 'beyond the year, in the year before', giving rise to adverbial **peruti* (Gk. πέρυσι 'last year', Arm. *herow*, OIc. *(í) fjǫrð*, OIr. *ónn-urid* 'since last year') with irregular deletion of the second vowel already in PIE.

PIE *ĝneu̯ >> *ĝnu

PIE **ō ĝneu̯* (loc.) yields **ōĝnu* > YAv. *ā-(x)šnu-* '(extending) to the knees' (Janda 1997: 156).

For an example from the history of German note that OHG univerbated **hiu=t[ag]u* gives rise to shortened *hiutu* > MHG *hiute* > Modern German *heute* ‚today', and likewise MHG univerbated **hī=n[ah]t* yields Modern Bavarian *heint* 'this night, today', as noted already by Meillet (1912: 138f.).

(b) Univerbation of numeral-noun NPs. Cf. e.g.

PIE *dek̑m̥t- >> *dk̑m̥t-

PIE **du̯(é)i̯ih$_1$* plus **dek̑m̥tih$_1$* 'two tens' is reduced to **du̯íh$_1$dk̑m̥tih$_1$* in univerbation > PIE **u̯ih$_1$dk̑m̥tih$_1$* (by early dissimilation **du̯_dk̑_* → **Øu̯_dk̑_*) > PIE **u̯ih$_1$k̑m̥tih$_1$* by the PIE sound law **dk̑m̥* > **k̑m̥* (Mayrhofer 1986: 152).

PIE *dek̑om-t >> *dk̑om-t

PIE collective *t*-stem **dék̑om-t* in PIE **tríh$_2$ dek̑om-t* 'three tens' yields **trih$_2$dk̑om-t* by phonetic reduction in univerbation. The latter form is indirectly reflected in Proto-Tocharian **tärya-kæ* > B *täryāka* 'thirty'.[52]

Alternatively, one might think of attributing the irregular zero-grade in decad formations like PIE **trih$_2$ dk̑om-t* to intra-paradigmatic leveling of the zero-grade root of ablauting weak case forms, i.e., the first syllable of **dek̑om-t* would be aligned analogically with that of gen. **dk̑m̥-t-óh$_x$om* (Rau 2009: 16). But two observations argue for subsuming the transformation of univerbated PIE **tríh$_2$=dek̑om-t* 'three tens' into **tríh$_2$dk̑om-t* under the phenomenon of reduction in univerbation. First, the case of PIE **du̯ih$_1$dk̑m̥tih$_1$* > **du̯ih$_1$k̑m̥tih$_1$* would require the alleged intra-paradigmatic

---

52 Note that **d(e)k̑omt* is doubly marked as a collective (with both *-*t* and *-*h$_2$*) as **d(e)k̑omt-h$_2$* in Greek (κοντ α), just as the reflexes of PIE **k^{w}etu̯ór-h$_2$* > **k^{w}etu̯ṓr* (Goth *fidwor*) are doubly marked to yield Indic *catvā́r-i* and Tocharian B *śtwā́r-a* by adding the collective formant *-*h$_2$* anew.

leveling to be older than the PIE sound law *dḱm̥ > *ḱm̥, which would be odd given the later preservation of *deḱm̥- in non-univerbated forms. Second and more importantly, the irregular deletion of the first vowel in *deḱom-t is confined to the univerbation of cardinal decad formations. In this respect, this formation differs markedly from uncompounded *déḱm̥-t, which shows no trace of the same irregular vowel deletion. Thus uncompounded PIE ***deḱ***m̥tih$_1$ remains intact in Lith. *(dvì) dẽšimti* (reanalyzed as a fem. *i*-stem) and OCS (masc. *dŭva) desętĭ*, whereas the irregular vowel deletion is confined to the univerbated syntagm PIE *du̯ih$_1$***dḱ***m̥tih$_1$ (Lat. *vīgintī*, Av. *vīsaiti*). This clearcut dichotomy is straightforwardly accounted for by the envisaged reduction process, which is associated precisely with univerbation.

To conclude, the irregular zero grade in **tisres* and *k^w*etesres* provides no formal obstacle to their origin in appositional collocations PIE **tri/*k^w*et* *(h_1)ésores*. The irregular loss of the *o*-grade is to be subsumed under the more general phenomenon of irregular phonological reduction in univerbation.

WOMAN >> numeral female classifier

Syntagm	**Reduction in univerbation**
PIE **tri* *(h_1)esores* *(h_1)eḱu̯ōs*	**t(r)isres* *(h_1)eḱu̯ōs*
PIE k^w*et* *(h_1)esores* *(h_1)eḱu̯ōs*	*k^w*etesres* *(h_1)eḱu̯ōs*
'three/four steeds'	

9.2.2.1.2. The placement of the generic term MAN/WOMAN and adjectival conversion of apposed generic nouns

The placement of the generic term 'man/woman' between the numeral and the counted object (Latin *trēs* ***virī*** *epulōnēs*) calls for comment. At first sight, it seems to contradict the above-claimed Indo-European tendency for unextended hyperonyms to follow their host. On closer inspection, however, the preposing of the generic noun before the head noun can be accounted for by adjectival conversion (cf. §4.2.3.).

Before addressing this question, it will first be useful to discuss the displacement of the generic noun. In the domain of counting, the presence of a cardinal as determiner causes the term for man and woman to be preposed, cf.

Postposed 'man/woman'	**Preposed numeral + 'man/woman' construction**
Latin X + ***mās/vir***, Oscan X + **niir** Latin *agnum* ***mārem*** (Fest. p. 204 Lindsay) Oscan *minat-eís* ***ner-eís*** (Rix 2002: Cp 25)	Latin *trēs* ***virī*** *epulōnēs* (Liv. 33.42.1)
Hittite *išhaš**šara-*** 'mistress'	Vedic *ti-**sró** devī́s* 'three goddesses' (RV 1.13,9)

Interestingly, the situation found in ancient Indo-European languages resembles that found in modern Bengali. As exemplified below, the unmarked position of apposed Bengali nouns is after the host noun. The same goes for the classifier if used as a definite marker, cf. Bengali *śromik-**jon*** def. 'the worker', *śromik-car-**jon***, def. 'the four workers'. By contrast, if used as an indefinite determiner phrase, the numeral plus classifier must precede the head noun, hence *car-jon śromik* 'four labourers' (Dasgupta 1983: 12):

Postposed	**Preposed**
Bengali *śromik-**jon*** definite 'the worker' *śromik-car-**jon*** definite 'the four workers'	*car-**jon** śromik* indefinite 'four labourers'

Thus, both Latin and Bengali alike attest to a rule which interposes apposed nouns between a cardinal number and the counted noun. This special rule can most straightforwardly be accounted for by postulating the adjectival conversion of the apposed noun and appealing to the default pre-head position of adjectives in Latin and Bengali.

In general, the adjectival zero-conversion of appositional nouns is a demonstrably widespread phenomenon in Indo-European languages. It typically occurs

- with nouns expressing abstract qualities, e.g., French *bête* 'stupid' ultimately from Lat. *bēstia* 'wild animal, ferocity', German *schade* 'pity, pitiful' ultimately from the MHG substantive *schade* 'damage', and Greek ψεῦδος 'false' from the substantive ψεῦδος 'lie';

- with quantifying abstracts: Latin *omnis* 'whole, all, every' from **op-ni-* 'entirety', Latin *potis* 'capable' from **pot-i-* 'master, capacity', Greek πολύς 'much, many' from **polh$_1$-u-* 'multitude';
- and with concrete generic nouns such as 'man' and 'woman', e.g. in Latin *mās* and *fēmina* (cf. *ThLL* 6.462f., s.v. *fēmina* II *dē animālibus ferē adiectīvī locō*).

The desubstantival origin of these words is indicated by their morphology–e.g., the acrostatic accent-ablaut class of πολύς or the substantival stem class (*s*-stem ψεῦδος, *(n)i*-stem abstract *omnis*)–and in general by their etymology (e.g. French *bête* < Latin *bēstia*).

Note the incipient character of the conversion. Many of the desubstantival adjectives are pseudo-adjectives, as indicated by their morphological defectivity (lack of gradation) and by syntactic constraints, e.g. exclusion of attributive use (German *schade*, Latin *potis*).

Languages such as Greek, which positionally distinguish preposed adjectives and postposed appositional substantives, likewise hint at the adjectival conversion of a noun by its leftward relocation. Thus, Ancient Greek, while postposing appositional nouns, e.g., ὄνομα **ψεῦδος** καὶ ἀληθὲς (Plato *Cra.* 385c), prefers the pre-head position in παράδοξόν τε καὶ **ψεῦδος** ὄνομα (Plato *Plt.* 281a). And Old Latin, despite its clear preference for postposing appositional *fēmina*, begins to prepose *fēmina* in ***fēminis*** *būbus* (Varro *R.* 2.1.17), *mās et* ***fēmina*** *aquila* (Varro *L.* 8.7).

9.3. Conclusion

The foregoing discussion establishes two points.

First, Proto-Indo-European shows a strong predilection towards postposing generic appositional substantives. The connection in Indo-European between postposing and OV word order is confirmed by typological comparison and can be accounted for by left-branching semantic subordination.

Second, there is a continuity between apposed generic nouns on the phraseological level in ancient Indo-European and nominal classifiers on the syntactic level in Modern Indo-Aryan. The case of the generic terms for 'man' and 'woman' illustrates both the beginning and the end of the grammaticalization of nominal classifiers. It demonstrates that the often claimed interface between lexicon and syntax is not just an abstract postulation but a concrete reality.

Abbreviations

BDB	*The Brown-Driver-Briggs Hebrew and English Lexicon*, by Francis Brown, with the cooperation of S. R. Driver and Charles A. Briggs. Peabody, Mass. ^{3}1997: Hendrickson Publishers.
CHD-P	Hans G. Güterbock, Harry A. Hoffner, *Chicago Hittite Dictionary, The Hittite Dictionary of the Oriental Institute of the University of Chicago.* Volume P. Chicago: Oriental Institute Univ. of Chicago 1997.
HW^2 1-3	Johannes Friedrich, Annelies Kammenhuber, *Hethitisches Wörterbuch*. Zweite, völlig neubearbeitete Auflage auf der Grundlage der edierten hethitischen Texte. Heidelberg: Carl Winter 1991ff.
LLP	*Lexicon Linguae Palaeoslovenicae (Slovník Jazyka Staroslověnského)*. Prague: Academia, Nakl. Československé Akad. Věd. 1958ff.
ThLL	*Thesaurus Linguae Latinae*. Munich: Saur Verlag.

References

AIKHENVALD, ALEXANDRA Y.
2000 *Classifiers: A Typology of Noun Categorization Devices*. Oxford: Oxford University Press.

ASHTON, E. O.
^{15}1970 *Swahili Grammar*. London: Longman.

BÁRCZI, GÉZA
2001 *Geschichte der ungarischen Sprache*. Innsbruck: Innsbrucker Beiträge zur Sprachwissenschaft.

BARTONĚK, ANTONÍN
2003 *Handbuch des mykenischen Griechisch*. Heidelberg: Carl Winter.

BENVENISTE, ÉMILE
1934 "Un nom indo-européen de la «femme»." *Bulletin de la Société de Linguistique* 35. 104-106.

BLACK, CHERYL A.
2000 *Quiegolani Zapotec Syntax*. Dallas: SIL International and University of Texas at Arlington.

CARDONA, GEORGE & DHANESH JAIN (eds.)
2003 *The Indo-Aryan languages*. London and New York: Routledge. (*Routledge Language Family Series* 2)

COWGILL, WARREN
1957 "Old Irish *teoir* and *cetheoir*." *Language* 33. 341-345. (= *The Collected Writings of Warren Cowgill*. Edited with an Introduction by Jared S. Klein, 277-280. Ann Arbor, New York: Beech Stave Press.)

CRAIG [GRINEVALD], COLETTE
1986 "Jacaltec noun classifiers, a study in language and culture." In: Colette Craig (ed.), *Noun Classes and Categorization*, 263-293. Amsterdam, Philadelphia: John Benjamins. (= TSL 7)
2000 "A morphosyntactic typology of classifiers." In: Senft 2000, 50-92.

CRUSE, D. A.
1975 "Hyponymy and lexical hierarchy." *Archivum Linguisticum* 6. 26-31.

DASGUPTA, PROBAL
1983 "On the Bangla classifier /Ta/, its penumbra, and definiteness." *Indian Linguistics* 44: 11-25.
2003 "Bangla." In: Cardona & Jain (eds), 351-390.

DELBRÜCK, BERTHOLD
1900 *Vergleichende Syntax der indogermanischen Sprachen*. Strassburg. Dritter Theil. Strassburg: Karl J. Trübner.

DIEWALD, GABRIELE
1997 *Grammatikalisierung. Eine Einführung in Sein und Werden grammatischer Formen.* Tübingen: Max Niemeyer Verlag.

DIXON, ROBERT M. W.
1977 *A Grammar of Yidiŋ*. Cambridge: Cambridge University Press.
2002 *Australian languages. Their nature and development*. Cambridge: Cambridge University Press.

DIXON, ROBERT M. W. & ALEXANDRA Y. AIKHENVALD
1999 *The Amazonian languages*. Cambridge: Cambridge University Press.

EHELOLF, HANS
1936 "Hethitisch-akkadische Wortgleichungen." *Zeitschrift für Assyriologie* N. F. 9 (Band 43), 170-195.

EPPS, PATIENCE
2007 "Birth of a noun classification system: the case of Hup," in: W. Leo Wetzels (ed.), *Language Endangerment and Endangered Languages: Linguistic and Anthropological Studies with Special Emphasis on the Languages and Cultures of the Andean-Amazonian Border Area.* 107-127. Indigenous Languages of Latin America series (ILLA). Publications of the Research School of Asian, African, and Amerindian Studies (CNWS). Leiden University.

EICHNER, HEINER
1973 "Die Etymologie von heth. *mehur*." *Münchener Studien zur Sprachwissenschaft* 31. 53-107.
1992 "Anatolian." In: *Indo-European Numerals*. Edited by Jadranka Gvozdanović, 29-96. Berlin, New York: Mouton, de Gruyter.

ESKA, JOSEPH F.
1989 *Towards an interpretation of the Hispano-Celtic inscription of Botorrita*. Innsbruck: Innsbrucker Beiträge zur Sprachwissenschaft.
1994[95] "Rethinking the evolution of Celtic constituent configuration." *Münchener Studien zur Sprachwissenschaft* 55. 7-39.

FORSSMAN, BERNHARD
2000 "Altindoarisch *prādúḥ* ‚sichtbar, erkennbar'." In: Almut Hintze & Eva Tichy (eds.), *Anusantatyai*. Festschrift für Johanna Narten zum 70. Geburtstag. Dettelbach: J. H. Röll. 39-54.

GESENIUS, WILHELM
1962 *Hebräisches und aramäisches Handwörterbuch über das Alte Testament*. Unveränderter Neudruck der 1915 erschienenen 17. Auflage. Berlin, Göttingen, Heidelberg: Springer-Verlag.

GIVÓN, TALMY
2000-2001 *Syntax*. Volume I. Amsterdam, Philadelphia: John Benjamins.

GOSWAMI, GOLOK CHANDRA & JYOTIPRAKASH TAMULI
2003 "Asamiya." In: Cardona & Jain (eds), 391-443.

GREENE, DAVID
1992 "Celtic." In: *Indo-European Numerals*. Edited by Jadranka Gvozdanović, 497-554. Berlin, New York: Mouton, de Gruyter.

GREGORES, EMMA & JORGE A. SUÁREZ
1967 *A Description of Colloquial Guaraní*. The Hague, Paris: Mouton.

GRINEVALD, COLETTE
2002 "Making sense of nominal classification systems." In: Ilse Wischer and Gabriele Diewald, *New Reflections on Grammaticalization*, 259-275. Amsterdam, Philadelphia: John Benjamins.

GRODDEK, DETLEV
2004 *Eine althethitische Tafel des KI.LAM-Festes*. München: Peniope, Anja Gärtig Verlag. (= *International Journal of Diachronic Linguistics and Linguistic Reconstruction*, Supplement 1)

GÜLDEMANN, TOM
1999 "Head-initial meets head-final: nominal suffixes in eastern and southern Bantu from a historical perspective." *Studies in African Linguistics* 28 (1). 49-91.

GÜTERBOCK, HANS GUSTAV
1956 "The deeds of Šuppiluliuma as told by his son, Muršili II." *Journal of Cuneiform Studies* 10.2, 41-68; 10.3, 75-98; 10.4, 107-130.

HACKSTEIN, OLAV
2003 "Apposition and word-order typology in Indo-European." In: Brigitte Bauer and Georges-Jean Pinault (eds.), *Festschrift for Werner Winter*, 131-152. Berlin, New York: Mouton de Gruyter.

2006 "La langue poétique indo-européenne: archaïsme et renouvellement dans les théonymes." In: *La langue poétique indo-européenne. Actes du Colloque de travail de la Société des Études Indo-Européennes*, 95-108. Edited by Georges-Jean Pinault & Daniel Petit. Leuven: Peeters.

HAGENBUCHNER, ALBERTINE
1989 *Die Korrespondenz der Hethiter*. Texte der Hethiter 16. Heidelberg: Carl Winter.

HEBERLEIN, FRIEDRICH
1996 "Über 'enge' Appositionen." In: Hannah Rosén (ed.), *Aspects of Latin. Papers from the Seventh International Colloquium on Latin Linguistics*, 343-359. Innsbruck: Institut für Sprachwissenschaft.

HEINE, BERND
1976 *A Typology of African Languages Based on the Order of Meaningful Elements.* Berlin: Dietrich Reimer. (= Kölner Beiträge zur Afrikanistik Band 4)

HEINE, BERND & TANIA KUTEVA
2002 *World Lexicon of Grammaticalization.* Cambridge: Cambridge University Press.

HEINE, BERND & MECHTHILD REH
1984 *Grammaticalization and Reanalysis in African Languages.* Hamburg: Helmut Buske Verlag.

HILLER, STEFAN
1986 "Tiernamen." In: Hiller, Stefan und Oswald Panagl 1986: *Die frühgriechischen Texte aus mykenischer Zeit.* Darmstadt: Wissenschaftliche Buchgesellschaft. 257-260.

HOFFNER, HARRY ANGIER
1997 *The Laws of the Hittites.* Leiden, New York, Köln: Brill.

HOFFNER, HARRY A.
2007 "Aspects of the Hittite system of numbering." In: *Festschrift in Honor of Belkıs Dinçol and Ali Dinçol.* Edited by Metin Alparslan, Meltem Doğan-Alparslan, Hasan Peker. İstanbul: Ege Yayınları. 327-340.

HOFFNER, HARRY A. & CRAIG MELCHERT
2008 *A Grammar of the Hittite Language.* Part I. Winona Lake: Eisenbrauns.

HOPPER, PAUL J. & ELIZABETH CLOSS TRAUGOTT
2003 *Grammaticalization.* Second edition. Cambridge: Cambridge University Press.

JANDA, MICHAEL
1997 *Über "Stock und Stein".* Dettelbach: J. H. Röll. (= MSS, Beiheft 18)
1999 "Zur Herkunft von homerisch ὄαρ." In: Sigrid Deger-Jalkotzy, Stefan Hiller, Oswald Panagl (Hrsg.), *Floreant Studia Mycenaea.* Wien: Verlag der Österreichischen Akademie der Wissenschaften. 315-324.
2008 "Häuser des Mondes: Ein indoiranisches Mythenfragment im avestischen Hymnus an Tištriia-Sirius." In: [*Chomolangma,*] *Demawend und Kasbek. Festschrift für Roland Bielmeier zu seinem 65. Geburtstag.* Band II: Chomolangma. Herausgegeben von Brigitte Huber, Marianne Volkert und Paul Widmer. Halle, Saale: International Institute for Tibetan and Buddhist Studies. 483-503.

KIM, RONALD
2005 "Ossetic *silæ/syl* and the Indo-Iranian word for 'female'." *International Journal of Diachronic Linguistics and Linguistic Reconstruction* 2, 2. 123-168.
2008 "The Celtic feminine numerals '3' and '4' revisited." In: *Keltische Forschungen* 3. 143-167.

KING, ALAN R. & BEGOTXU OLAIZOLA ELORDI
1996 *Colloquial Basque. A Complete Language Course*. London: Routledge.
KISS, KATALIN É.
1987 *Configurationality in Hungarian*. Dordrecht, Boston, Lancaster, Tokyo: D. Reidel Publishing Company.
KÜHNER, RAPHAEL & FRIEDRICH HOLZWEISSIG
1912 *Ausführliche Grammatik der lateinischen Sprache. Erster Teil: Elementar-, Formen- und Wortlehre*. 2. Auflage. Hannover. Nachdruck Darmstadt 1994: Wissenschaftliche Buchgesellschaft.
KÜHNER, RAPHAEL & CARL STEGMANN
1955 *Ausführliche Grammatik der lateinischen Sprache*. Zweiter Teil: Satzlehre. Hannover: Hahnsche Buchhandlung.
LA ROCHE, JACOB
1893 *Homerische Untersuchungen*. Zweiter Theil. Leipzig: B. G. Teubner.
LASS, ROGER
2000 "Which end is your head on? Typological remarks on Modern Persian." In: Christiane Dalton-Puffer & Nikolaus Ritt (eds.), *Words: structure, meaning, function. A Festschrift for Dieter Kastovsky*, 175-186. Berlin, New York: Mouton de Gruyter.
LAWRENZ, BIRGIT
1993 *Apposition, Begriffsbestimmung und syntaktischer Status*. Tübingen: Gunter Narr.
LEDO-LEMOS, FRANCISCO JOSÉ
2000 *Femininum Genus. A Study on the Origins of the Indo-European Feminine Grammatical Gender*. München: Lincom.
LEHMANN, CHRISTIAN
1988 "Towards a typology of clause linkage." In: John Haiman & Sandra A. Thompson (eds.), *Clause Combining in Grammar and Discourse*, 181-225. Amsterdam, Philadelphia: Benjamins.
2000 "On the German numeral classifier system." In: Schaner-Wolles, Chris, John R. Rennison & Friedrich Neubarth (eds.), *Naturally! Linguistic studies in honour of Wolfgang Ulrich Dressler presented on the occasion of his 60th birthday*, 249-253. Torino: Rosenberg & Sellier.
LEUMANN, MANU, JOHAN B. HOFMANN & ANTON SZANTYR
1965 *Lateinische Grammatik*. Band II: Syntax. Munich: Beck.
LÜHR, ROSEMARIE
1996 *Neuhochdeutsch, eine Einführung in die Sprachwissenschaft*. 5. durchgesehene Auflage. Munich: Fink Verlag.
MAYRHOFER, MANFRED
1986 *Indogermanische Grammatik*. Heidelberg: Carl Winter.
MEILLET, ANTOINE
1912 "L'évolution des formes grammaticales." *Scientia (Rivista di scienza)*, vol. 12, no. 26, 6. 130-148.
MERINGER, RUDOLF
1904 "Wörter und Sachen." *Indogermanische Forschungen* 16. 101-196.

MOTTA, FILIPPO
1993 "Die Namenformeln im Altkeltischen." In: *Lengua y cultura en la Hispania prerromana*, ed. by J. Untermann, F. Villar, 697-718 Salamanca: Ediciones Universidad de Salamanca.

NEUMANN, GÜNTER
1982 "Die Konstruktionen mit Adjectiva genetivalia in den luwischen Sprachen." In: Erich Neu (ed.), *Investigationes Philologicae et Comparativae. Gedenkschrift für Heinz Kronasser*, 149-161. Wiesbaden: Harrassowitz.
1993 "Neue Erkenntnisse zur lykischen Sprache. Appositionen zu Personennamen." In: Jürgen Borchhardt & Gerhard Dobesch (ed.), *Akten des II. Internationalen Lykien-Symposions*, Bd. I, 35-38. Vienna: Verlag der Österreichischen Akademie der Wissenschaften.

NUSSBAUM, ALAN
1986 *Head and Horn in Indo-European*. Berlin, New York: Walter de Gruyter.

OETTINGER, NORBERT
1986 "Awestisch *hāirišī-*." *Indogermanische Forschungen* 91. 116-128.

PANAGL, OSWALD
2006 "Notizen zur Syntax der neuen thebanischen Linear B-Tafeln." In: Sigrid Deger-Jalkotzy & Oswald Panagl (eds.), *Die neuen Linear B-Texte aus Theben*, 149-157. Vienna: Verlag der Österreichischen Akademie der Wissenschaften.

PECCHIOLI DADDI, FRANCA
1982 *Mestieri, professioni e dignità nell' Anatolia ittita*. Roma: Edizioni dell' Ateneo. (= Incunabula Graeca 79)

PINAULT, GEORGES-JEAN
1994 "Aspects du bouddhisme pratiqué au nord du désert du Taklamakan, d'après les documents tokhariens." In: *Bouddhisme et cultures locales*. Actes du colloque franco-japonais de septembre 1991 édités par Fukui Fumimasa et Gérard Fussman, 85-113. Paris: École française d' Extrême-Orient.
1998 "Economic and administrative documents in Tocharian B from the Berezovsky and Petrovsky collections." *Manuscripta Orientalia* Vol. 4. No. 4 (December 1998), 3-20. St. Petersburg, Helsinki.

PINAULT, GEORGES-JEAN , GENG SHIMIN & JENS PETER LAUT
2004 "Neue Ergebnisse der *Maitrisimit*-Forschung (II): Struktur und Inhalt des 26. Kapitels." *Studies on the Inner Asian Languages* 19. 29-94. (Kyoto: The Society of Central Eurasian Studies)

PRIMUS, BEATRICE
2001 "Word order typology." In: *Language Typology and Language Universals. Handbuch für Sprachwissenschaft und Kommunikationswissenschaft*. Band 2.2, 855-873. Berlin, New York: Mouton de Gruyter.

RAU, JEREMY
2009 *Indo-European Nominal Morphology: the Decads and the Caland System*. Innsbruck: Innsbrucker Beiträge zur Sprachwissenschaft.

RIEKEN, ELISABETH
1999 *Untersuchungen zur nominalen Stammbildung des Hethitischen.* Wiesbaden: Harrassowitz.

RIX, HELMUT
2002 *Sabellische Texte.* Heidelberg: Winter.

SCHINDLER, JOCHEM
1979 Review of "Jean Kellens, Les noms-racines de l'Avesta. Wiesbaden, Reichert 1974." *Die Sprache* 25. 57-60.

SCHMIDT, JOHANNES
1889 *Die Pluralbildungen der indogermanischen Sprachen.* Weimar: Hermann Böhlau.

SCHMIDT, KLAUS T.
1998 "Interdisciplinary research on Central Asia: the decipherment of the West Tocharian captions of a cycle of mural paintings of the life of Buddha in cave 110 in Qizil." *Die Sprache* 40.1. 72-81.
1999 "Beobachtungen zur tocharischen Landwirtschaftsterminologie." *Die Sprache* 41.1. 1-23.

SCHWYZER, EDUARD
1947 *Zur Apposition.* Abhandlungen der Deutschen Akademie der Wissenschaften zu Berlin, Jahrgang 1945/6, phil.-hist. Klasse Nr. 3. Berlin: Akademie-Verlag.

SEILER, HANSJAKOB
1960 *Relativsatz, Attribut und Apposition.* Wiesbaden: Harrassowitz.

SENFT, GUNTER
1996 *Classificatory Particles in Kilivila.* Oxford: Oxford University Press.

SENFT, GUNTER (ED.)
1999 *Systems of Nominal Classification.* Cambridge: Cambridge University Press.

SIEG, EMIL, WILHELM SIEGLING & WILHELM SCHULZE
1931 *Tocharische Grammatik.* Göttingen: Vandenhoeck & Ruprecht.

SINGER, ITAMAR
1995 ""Our god" and "their God" in the Anitta Text." In: *Atti del II Congresso Internazionale di Ittitologia*, 343-349. Pavia: Gianni Iuculano Editore.

SNEDDON, JAMES
1996 *Indonesian, a Comprehensive Grammar.* London: Routledge.
2003 *The Indonesian Language: its History and Role in Modern Society.* Sydney: UNSW Press.

SOUČEK, VLADIMÍR
1959 "Die hethitischen Feldertexte." *Archiv Orientální* 27. 5-43.

STARKE, FRANK
1977 *Die Funktionen der dimensionalen Kasus und Adverbien im Althethitischen.* Wiesbaden: Otto Harrassowitz. (= *Studien zu den Boğazköy-Texten* 23)
1990 *Untersuchung zur Stammbildung des keilschrift-luwischen Nomens.* Wiesbaden: Otto Harrassowitz. (= *Studien zu den Boğazköy-Texten* 31)

STIFTER, DAVID
2006 *Sengoidelc. Old Irish for Beginners.* Syracuse: University Press.

TAYLOR, ANN
1994 "The change from SOV to SVO in Ancient Greek." *Language Variation and Change* 6.1. 1-37.

THURNEYSEN, RUDOLF
1946 *A Grammar of Old Irish.* Revised and enlarged edition with a supplement. Translated from the German by D. A. Binchy and Osborn Bergin. Reprinted 1980. Dublin: The Dublin Institute for Advanced Studies.

TRASK, R. LARRY
1997 *The History of Basque.* London, New York: Routledge.

WATKINS, CALVERT
1971 [1973] "Hittite and Indo-European studies: the denominative statives in *-ē-*." *Transactions of the Philological Society* 1971. 51-93.
1975 "Die Vertretung der Laryngale in gewissen morphologischen Kategorien in den indogermanischen Sprachen Anatoliens." In: *Flexion und Wortbildung. Akten der V. Fachtagung der Indogermanischen Gesellschaft.* Wiesbaden: Reichert. 358-378.
1976 "Towards Proto-Indo-European syntax: problems and pseudo-problems." In: S. Steever, C. Walker, and S. Mufwene (eds), *Papers from the parasession on diachronic syntax*, 305-326. Chicago: Chicago Linguistics Society.

WILKINS, DAVID P.
1989 *Mparntwe Arrernte (Aranda): Studies in the Structure and Semantics of Grammar.* PhD thesis, Australian National University, Canberra.
2001 "Ants, ancestors and medicine: a semantic and pragmatic account of classifier constructions in Arrernte (Central Australia)." In: Senft 2000, 147-215.

WINTER, WERNER
1987 "Tocharian B *ñakte*, A *ñkät* 'god': two nouns, their derivatives, their etymology." *Journal of Indo-European Studies* 15. 297-325.

ZAVALA, ROBERTO
2000 "Multiple classifier systems in Acatec (Mayan)." In: Senft 2000: 114-146.

Index of Subjects

Index of of non-Indo-European Languages

Index of Words

Tocharian

Proto-Indo-European